D1622544

Winning
Negotiations
That Preserve
Relationships

The Results-Driven Manager Series

The Results-Driven Manager series collects timely articles from *Harvard Management Update* and *Harvard Management Communication Letter* to help senior to middle managers sharpen their skills, increase their effectiveness, and gain a competitive edge. Presented in a concise, accessible format to save managers valuable time, these books offer authoritative insights and techniques for improving job performance and achieving immediate results.

Other books in the series:

Managing Yourself for the Career You Want

Teams That Click

Presentations That Persuade and Motivate

Face-to-Face Communications for Clarity and Impact

A Timesaving Guide

THE RESULTS-DRIVEN MANAGER

Winning Negotiations That Preserve Relationships

Harvard Business School Press

Boston, Massachusetts

Copyright 2004 Harvard Business School Publishing Corporation

All rights reserved

Printed in the United States of America
08 07 06 05 04   5 4 3 2 1

Library of Congress Cataloging-in-Publication Data

The results-driven manager: winning negotiations that preserve
    relationships.
        p.   cm. — (The results-driven manager series)
    Added t.p. title: Winning negotiations that preserve relationships.
    Articles previously published in Harvard Management Update and
    Harvard Management Communication Letter.
        ISBN 1-59139-348-5 (alk. paper)
        1. Negotiation in business. I. Title: Winning negotiations that
    preserve relationships. II. Harvard Business School Press III. Series.
    HD58.6.W566 2004
    658.4′052—dc22
                                                        2003019404

The paper used in this publication meets the requirements of the American National Standard for Permanence of Paper for Publications and Documents in Libraries and Archives Z39.48-1992.

Contents

Contents

Negotiating Across Cultures

Winning Negotiations That Preserve Relationships

Introduction

* * *

Quick: When you think about the word *negotiation*, what comes to mind? Do you picture two teams of high-level, aggressive VIPs sitting across a vast table from one another, armed with elaborate files and briefcases and determined to outwit each other? Certainly some negotiations take place in this sort of setting and have this competitive, adversarial quality. But the best negotiations are collaborative—they take place under the assumption that the parties' relationship is equally as important as the details of the deal.

Negotiations that preserve relationships generate valuable business results. They enable you to:

- Arrive at surprisingly creative solutions to problems

- Build skills that make future negotiations easier and more successful

- Strengthen valuable working relationships

- Keep interpersonal conflicts from escalating

- Strike deals that benefit both your own company and the other party's firm

By contrast, a lack of negotiation skills can put you at a huge disadvantage on the job—as well as damage your company. To get a taste of the kind of trouble that badly handled bargaining can lead to, imagine the obverse of each of the five examples in the bulleted list above. It's hard to decide what's worse: forging deals that put your company at a disadvantage? seeing workplace conflicts balloon out of control? finding that your relationships with colleagues have deteriorated beyond repair?

Clearly, skillful negotiating with an eye toward preserving relationships pays big dividends. It also takes some understanding and practice.

What *Is* Negotiation, Anyway?

Most of us engage in numerous negotiations every day—in both the workplace and at home. Indeed, anytime we interact with colleagues, family members, friends, neighbors, and store clerks, we may be engaging in negotiating. For example, in one day, you might:

- Dicker with the boss for a raise

- Try to reach terms with your 10-year-old about how much TV she can watch

- Work out pricing and delivery terms with a potential new overseas supplier

- Put an offer in on a house

- Figure out which of your direct reports are going to handle which tasks in an upcoming project

- Bargain with senior management for the budget allocations you need to accomplish your departmental goals for the year

But what *is* negotiation, exactly? And why is it increasingly important for managers who want to get the best possible results in today's workplace? Negotiation isn't about outwitting or taking advantage of others. It's about arriving at a shared solution to a problem—a solution that benefits all parties involved. It's also about a lot more than just getting the best possible price on a deal. The most effective negotiations result in mutually beneficial, enduring relationships in which the parties trust one another and share expectations about how their deals will work out in practice as well as on paper.

Moreover, the most successful bargainers strike deals that satisfy a broad range of interests beyond concerns about price. Here's one example: A consultant who's just getting into the business discusses the possibility of taking on a project for a potential new client that has high prestige in its industry but a limited budget. The two sides agree to a discounted fee. The arrangement satisfies some of the consultant's nonfinancial interests—such as building up his clientele with high-profile names and having the opportunity to put the "word-of-mouth" engine in motion. And the deal enables the client to "try out" the consultant and thus lower the risk of investing in consulting services while under the constraints of a tight budget. Though the two parties discuss and work out financial terms, the final details of the deal address far more than monetary concerns.

Relationships and Collaboration

Characterized by a broad range of players and interests, workplace negotiations thus take place within a complex web of human relationships—among employees, customers, partner companies, even competitors.

To begin improving your negotiation skills, think of negotiating as a process—not a one-time event. This process creates a delicate balance between competition and cooperation and, if well handled, fosters long-term, positive relationships. In fact, some experts refer to the connections forged by skillful negotiation as *strategic relationships*.

In strategic relationships, people are open with one another; they share knowledge and feel free to express their emotions. They also trust each other to protect one another's interests as well as their own. An atmosphere of collaboration and community pervades the relationship, and the parties share the understanding that the relationship is ongoing. The participants listen intently to one another and ask frequent questions—viewing each other as partners rather than adversaries.

Why the emphasis on relationships? As Rebecca Saunders writes in "How to Negotiate an Alliance You Can Live With," "Strategic alliances dominate today's business landscape. Some company is always announcing agreements with its supply-chain partners, competitors—even former customers." Add joint ventures, partnerships, mergers, and acquisitions to the picture, and you can see even more evidence for the primacy of relationships in business.

In addition, many businesspeople have discovered that command-and-control hierarchies and regimentation don't necessarily improve a company's productivity, profitability, or efficiency. Rather, companies encourage a lot more creativity in their workforces by creating "flatter" decision-making structures. And, along with creativity and flatter decision making come additional opportunities for conflict in the ranks. When more people throughout a company are making decisions rather than simply following orders, their mutual interdependency increases. Put another way, today we need more input and cooperation from one another to fulfill our job responsibilities.

Flatter organizational structures constitute just one source of increased conflict and misunderstanding in the workplace. As many companies extend their operations into countries around the globe, the cultural differences they encounter can make it even harder to establish the strong relationships required for successful negotiation.

All this isn't to say that relationships are more important than hard-core business results. As Sy, Barbara, and Daryl Landau maintain in "Negotiating When Your Job Depends on It":

> In organizations, both results and relationships are important; organizations exist to produce results through the combined efforts of their members. Problems should be solved in ways that promote the competition of ideas while encouraging the cooperation of people. This is the essence of collaboration.

The four sections of this volume walk you through the major challenges of negotiating to preserve relationships:

- establishing a collaborative context for bargaining

- forging and sustaining solid strategic partnerships

- negotiating under high-pressure conditions (such as during intense conflicts or with an especially hard-nosed counterpart)

- steering clear of the pitfalls associated with cross-cultural negotiation.

Let's take a closer look at each of these themes.

Negotiating Collaboratively

How do you begin establishing a collaborative atmosphere for negotiating? Understand the difference between *positions* and *interests*. The first article in this section, "The Best Negotiation Advice: From Before You Sit Down to After You've Struck a Deal," defines *position* as your stance on an issue—for example, "I won't take less than $3,000 for my used car." *Interests*, by contrast, relate to the desires, needs, and hopes that have given rise to your position. In this case, your interests might include seeing your beloved old car go to a new owner who appreciates it, making enough money on the sale to buy a different sort of vehicle, and so forth.

When people bargain from positions, they tend to get locked into a tiresome offer-and-counteroffer exchange. Each side tries to arrive at a final number closer to its initial proposal. The participants expend more effort on asserting and defending their successive positions than on arriving at a solution that's optimal for both parties.

When you negotiate based on interests, however—digging into the desires, needs, and hopes behind the positions—you stand a better chance of arriving at a creative solution that you didn't anticipate, and that proves far more satisfying to each party.

In "How to Get What You Want: Do's and Don't's of Successful Negotiation," Roger J. Volkema affirms the importance of a collaborative bargaining style. Collaborators, he maintains, are "most likely to achieve that elusive win-win negotiating success." The key to collaborative negotiation? Clarify your own needs and goals. And try to understand the other side's interests by asking questions—being sure to test your understanding through paraphrasing and summarizing. Resist any urge to "tell the other side what a good deal it is getting."

"Win-Win with Mark Gordon" delves further into the secrets of successful collaborative negotiation, including the importance of getting away from positional thinking. Gordon raises the stakes by urging corporations to establish collaborative negotiation *systems*. Rather than focusing on individual deals, companies must consider "the whole universe of transactions that take place between [themselves] and other business entities." Organizations can assess their overall negotiating style and reinforce the desired collaborative style and attitudes through formal and informal incentives.

In "A Better Way to Negotiate," Tom Krattenmaker rounds out the section by offering seven potent tips for strengthening business alliances. His advice centers on ways to cultivate an atmosphere of collaboration. For example, Krattenmaker urges negotiators to imagine themselves united against a common challenge or problem—rather than engaged in a zero-sum contest in which one party's gain is the other's loss.

Krattenmaker also shares Gordon's opinion that organizations can do more to strengthen their negotiation systems. In his view, companies must become "more mindful of strategic relationships," paying special attention to the people they appoint as representatives: "You need someone who embodies the organization you represent." In today's environment, that person is *not* "a chest-thumper who calls comrades to arms and sets out to beat the opponent at all costs." Rather, "the ideal liaisons have a talent for cogent communicating and an ability to achieve and demonstrate understanding of the allies' needs."

Forging and Sustaining Strategic Partnerships

This section takes a closer look at the theme of strategic partnerships among companies as opposed to individuals. In "How to Negotiate an Alliance You Can Live With," Rebecca M. Saunders lays out a roadmap for getting a partner to agree to an alliance—and then hammering out the terms of the deal. The key? To figure out what your company could gain from a partnership and what assets it could provide in return.

To attract a partner, get everyone on your negotiating team to brainstorm a list of objectives and then prioritize them, identifying deal breakers. Compile a list of prospective partners by studying candidates' annual reports, press clippings, and public relations. If possible, talk with their customers and attend industry meetings at which their executives will speak. Court prospective partners with the goal of ultimately building a trusting relationship.

To work out the terms of an alliance, share information willingly, clearly state mutual goals and needs, and listen carefully so as to verify your assumptions. Equally important, ask questions—and don't rush. As in any long-term relationship, be willing to abandon unrealistic expectations.

In "Making Your Proposal Come Out on Top," Nick Wreden examines things from the other side's perspective—that of the company being approached by another firm to forge a possible strategic alliance. To boost your chances of being selected as a strategic partner, Wreden advises, create a proposal that makes it as difficult as possible for the "courting" company to eliminate you in the first round of reviews.

The key? Establish a disciplined process that enables you to avoid last-minute rushes—which only breed errors. With the prospective partner company's point of view in mind, analyze the prospect's requirements. Develop strategies, solutions, staffing requirements, and pricing possibilities. Outline timetables and responsibilities. Wreden defines all the components and qualities of a compelling proposal, and offers suggestions for personalizing the written presentation so that it appeals to your prospective partner's point of view.

The way you frame your proposal is just as important as which details you include in it. In "The Right Frame: Managing Meaning and Making Proposals," Marjorie Corman Aaron explains that effective framing—the deliberate highlighting of some aspects of a proposal—taps into mental models, our assumptions about how to behave under various conditions. The way you frame a proposal may determine the mental model your readers decide to follow.

Aaron offers an example: Suppose you're a VP of a small engineering company negotiating with a large general contractor regarding cost overruns. He's discussing every dime. You widen the frame by referring to the multimillion-dollar magnitude of the overall project—and note the savings your work generated in other areas.

Studies have shown that with this sort of positive framing—which highlights participants' actual or potential gains rather than losses—more negotiators reach agreements and view the outcomes as fair.

The next article in this section, Stephen Bernhut's "After the Deal Is Done: Four Keys to Managing an Alliance," examines the "heavy lifting" that comes *after* the ink has dried on a signed contract between partnering companies. No matter how strongly two companies agree on the "letter of the deal," the success of any strategic alliance hinges on the two parties' ability to manage their relationship day to day.

Bernhut describes the building blocks of a successful, sustainable alliance in terms of four practices: 1) *Make alliance management a core capability in your company* by institutionalizing the best alliance-management practices and building a "center of learning" where managers can learn about contracts, audits, and other practices. 2) *Build and manage trust* by ensuring that some of the people negotiating the alliance will also be managing it. Keep your commitments, and know your partner's goals. 3) *Audit the relationship* by gauging the alliance's "emotional health" as well as business and technical milestones. 4) *Develop a protocol for joint decision making* by creating a decision-making task force, listing the 20–50 most significant decisions that need to be made and identifying key stakeholders in these significant decisions.

Jeff Weiss concludes this section with "Negotiation as a Business Process," in which he offers additional guidelines for making negotiation a core competency in your organization. Weiss describes the five phases that a company must go through to institutionalize negotiation as a business process: 1) *Gain and sustain internal alignment* to ensure that negotiating teams receive consistent messages about how key decisions should be made. 2) *Provide instructions* specifying the key interests that must be satisfied in an upcoming negotiation, best alternatives to a negotiated deal, and relationship goals that must be achieved. 3) *Enable negotiating teams to prepare* by providing them with templates and other tools for analyzing the other side's interests. 4) *Conduct the negotiation* according to the company's established standards and procedures. 5) *Review and learn from the negotiation*, capturing lessons about what worked and what didn't.

Negotiating Under Pressure

In any negotiation aimed toward preserving relationships, you'll find plenty of challenges—but some negotiations are thornier than others. The articles in this section help you to bargain under particularly high-pressure circumstances. Anne Field starts things off with "How to Negotiate with a Hard-Nosed Adversary." Though she uses words like *opponent* and *adversary*, her advice offers important lessons to collaborative as well as competitive bargainers.

With careful preparation and the right game plan, Field says, even a relatively inexperienced negotiator can turn the tables on an aggressive counterpart. How? Start by getting to know the other party—engaging him or her in "some preliminary negotiating over a relatively minor element of the process, such as where to hold the discussion." Such early probing can give you a sense of just how competitive the other person will be during the actual negotiation. Most people, Field has observed, "*over*estimate how competitive their opponent will be."

Also plan comebacks and strategic moves ahead of time—when you're not unduly influenced or intimidated by the other person's aggressive stance. For example, if you think a long-time client is going to complain vociferously about your fees, research industry fees so that you can confidently stand by your pricing during the actual negotiation.

In addition to hard-nosed counterparts, intense workplace conflicts can make relationship-focused negotiations particularly difficult. Because conflicts catalyze powerful emotions, they can escalate out of control if you're not careful.

In "Negotiating When Your Job Depends on It," Nick Morgan describes an eight-step process for preventing conflicts from escalating. The steps include assessing the strengths of the other side's position as well as the weaknesses of your own position, listening so as to understand the full set of issues on the table, brainstorming win-win outcomes, and being willing to "give a little."

Though painful and complex, workplace conflicts also play an essential role in both personal and organizational growth, Morgan explains in "Transforming Negotiations." Morgan quotes experts Peter M. Kellett and Diana G. Dalton:

> Conflict is an integral part of . . . how organizations manage . . . the tensions between creativity and constraint. . . . Contemporary organizations thrive and keep their employees productive when they allow them the freedom to voice experiences and the participation that stimulates creativity. . . . [But] there is also a need for order—constraints— so creativity is directed at achieving organizational goals.

Kellett and Dalton further distinguish conflict from compromise:

> There are two major problems with compromise. The first occurs when mediation becomes indistinguishable from capitulation. The second transpires when parties are asked to compromise over matters of principle, which is like advocating a happy medium between truth and lies, freedom and slavery, peace and war. . . . Compromise produces results that are intermediate, lukewarm, mediocre, vague, average, and ordinary.

If conflict resolution isn't compromise, what it is? It's "collaboration to produce something new and creative—something transformational." Collaborative conflict resolution occurs when you listen carefully to both sides—to grasp the context of the conflict and the emotions involved. Dig out the underlying causes of the conflict: Does the difficulty stem from differences in personalities? emotions? hidden expectations? unresolved issues between the two parties? Once you understand the forces behind the situation, look for creative ways to build on common ground between you and the other party—and move toward resolution.

In "Expert Negotiating," Jeffrey Marshall's interview with negotiation veteran G. Richard Shell reveals additional tips for successful negotiating under pressure. Most important, be yourself: "If you're a very cooperative person, and you find yourself in a nail-biting, hard negotiation situation, the chances are that you won't be very successful. . . . [Consider turning] the negotiation over to someone else who is more competitive." In addition, "[though] it always helps to be in control of your emotions, it can also be effective to express them. . . . Use your temper, don't lose it."

Negotiating Across Cultures

Perhaps the toughest test of your negotiating skills comes with doing business abroad—when cultures clash and the potential for misunderstanding soars. In "How to Avoid Being the 'Ugly American' When Doing Business Abroad," Andrew Rosenbaum suggests developing sensitivity to three major aspects of cross-cultural bargaining: 1) *The rhythm of negotiations*. Know that not everyone values speed and directness. 2) *The dynamics of personal relationships*. In many cultures, people value relationships far more than the details of the deal. 3) *The depth of presentation*. In cultures that value detail, slick speeches and flashy PowerPoint presentations won't get you as far as having all the numbers—and knowing what they mean.

Rosenbaum continues the theme of intercultural bargaining in "How to Steer Clear of Pitfalls in Cross-Cultural Negotiation." He offers additional advice: 1) *Understand differences in decision-making styles*. For example, Americans value flexibility, whereas Japanese managers believe it is shameful to change a decision once they've made one. 2) *Establish common ground* by finding anything that will allow your foreign colleague to share something with you. 3) *Manage the negotiation.* For instance, if the other side repeatedly insists on its terms to tire you out, change the subject or use some other tactic to display your unwillingness to hurry the deal.

Negotiating to preserve relationships requires a lot more savvy and a deeper understanding of people than simple competitive bargaining does. But by mastering the art of collaboration and forging strategic partnerships with an eye toward sustaining those relationships, you'll begin striking more mutually beneficial deals. And by discovering how to negotiate under high-pressure circumstances—including across cultures—you'll hone your skills to an even sharper point.

Negotiating Collaboratively

. . .

Negotiations that preserve and strengthen workplace relationships hinge on collaboration rather than out-right competition. As the articles in this section reveal, collaborative bargainers understand each other's inter-ests—the desires, needs, and hopes that give rise to their positions on the issues up for discussion. Rather than arguing from rigid positions, they craft creative deals that appeal to both parties' interests.

Such negotiators also envision themselves as united with the "other side" against a common challenge or problem—rather than engaged in a bare-knuckled con-test in which one party's gain must be the other's loss. And instead of viewing negotiation as something that takes place only between individuals or teams, they strive to create effective negotiation *systems* in their companies. Such systems help managers throughout the company learn from one another's experiences and send a consistent message to strategic partners from other organizations.

The Best
Negotiation
Advice

From Before You Sit Down to
After You've Struck a Deal

• • •

Books on how to negotiate almost invariably begin with the same observation: That the reader, whether he or she realizes it, is constantly engaged in the N-activity—when buying or selling a house, of course, or dickering with the boss for a raise, but also, if less obviously, when trying to reach terms with the local ten-year-old on how much TV she may watch. While one might question some aspects of this assertion—do you really want to approach little Jessica exactly the same way you do plaid-pants Phil at the used car lot?—basically it's true, and in the workplace growing more so.

As employee expectations chip away at hierarchy, old notions of "Just tell 'em what to do" increasingly get supplanted by negotiation in deciding what a so-called subordinate will undertake, how, and by when. These days what enlightened businessperson would say to an important customer or supplier, "Here's the price—take it or leave it"? No, you're supposed to build a relationship, explore the other party's interests, and try to figure out where these may overlap with your own. To negotiate, in other words.

With the increased importance of the subject in mind, *Harvard Management Update* has surveyed a half-dozen of the guides to negotiating available at your local bookstore. We deliberately sought a wide variety of approaches, expecting, for example, to find collections of nasty tricks for clobbering the other guy that we could compare and contrast to more judicious counsel. Maybe it's just our bookstore, but what we turned up was a remarkable degree of consensus across books ranging from the Ur-text *Getting to Yes*—authors from the Harvard Negotiation Project, over two million copies in print—to *The Complete Idiot's Guide to Winning Through Negotiation*. What follows is a distillation of the best advice.

Before You Sit Down
with the Other Party

While preparing yourself beforehand is a good idea in most endeavors, in negotiating it's critical, lest you be immediately overwhelmed by the other side. You will need to prepare on two fronts: getting the right attitude, and gathering information on what your interests are and what the other party's might be.

The recommended attitude for negotiating is a bit clinical, detached, even selfless in a Zen sense. As *Getting to Yes* co-authors Roger Fisher and William Ury stress, you want to separate the people from the problem, and the first person to separate is yourself. Letting your feelings hang out over the bargaining table is like wearing a sign saying "Hey, it's okay to do weird emotional judo on me."

The imperative to plumb interests lies at the heart of what distinguishes enlightened negotiating from the other kind. What you want to avoid, the experts agree, is bargaining over, or from, positions. You know: "I'll give you a hundred bucks for it." "I wouldn't take less than $50." And so on, tiresomely and unimaginatively, offer and counteroffer, each side trying to arrive at a final number closer to its initial proposal. More effort goes into asserting and defending successive positions than arriving at a solution that's optimal for both parties.

In negotiating based on interests, by contrast, the point is to get beyond positions to uncover the desires, needs, and hopes that have given rise to those positions. Once the two parties have explored their respective interests together, they may well be able to arrive at an outcome not contemplated in either's initial offer but that satisfies each far better than the result of a long haggle.

In his book *Win-Win Negotiating*, Fred E. Jandt offers a nifty real-world example. A friend, a lawyer in solo practice, was approached by his secretary asking for a raise. She came armed with all sorts of objective data indicating that most legal secretaries in the area made 30% to 50% more than she did, and that it would cost him three years of the raise just to hire and train a replacement if she left. The trouble was, with a practice skewed toward public interest work—read "not that lucrative"—the lawyer couldn't afford the increased outlay.

But instead of countering with his own position ("The money just isn't there"), the enlightened lawyer asked her questions—the key technique in negotiating from interests—to get at what was behind her request. It turned out that she really did need more money to get by. He also found out that she liked working for him, didn't particularly want to go somewhere else, and would be happy to put in some extra time.

Which presented the opening for a win-win solution: The lawyer arranged for her to do part-time work for another attorney, and, to sweeten the bargain, offered her the free use of the word processor in their office. So equipped, as a free-lancer in her spare time she was able to earn an hourly rate five times what he was paying her, and three times the rate at other law firms. Working every other Saturday, she grossed more than she would have received from the raise, and kept the full-time job that she enjoyed.

In understanding your own interests, and in calculating what the books call your "negotiating power," the key is determining your best alternative to a negotiated agreement, usually abbreviated as BATNA (also BATANA). Where will you be left if you can't strike a deal? How can you satisfy your interests without the cooperation of the other party? Think hard about this. In negotiating to buy a car, for example, the better BATNA is probably not "Gee, I won't have the joy of owning this snazzy little roadster that I've had my heart set on," but rather something like "Well, my current car still runs fine, I'll save a ton of money, and maybe I can find a vehicle that's even more fun."

The stronger your BATNA, the greater your negotiating power. A standard illustration of the point: Who's better situated to ask the boss for a promotion, the woman with job offers from two other employers in her attaché case, or the woman without clear prospects elsewhere? Which suggests an important, if easy to overlook, step in preparing to bargain: Go out and improve your BATNA. Scrounge up the two job offers.

Once you've determined your BATNA, you can use it to help sharpen the guidelines you set for yourself in the negotiation and the proposals you may want to make in starting the discussions. Particularly for dealing with a party who's not inclined to interest-based bargaining, Jandt recommends a strategy called mini-max. (Fair warning: Some partisans of getting to you-know-what might consider this strategy too positional.) Ask yourself four questions:

1. What's the minimum you're prepared to accept? Consult your BATNA. How ready are you to fall back on it?

2. What's the maximum you can ask for without getting laughed out of the room?

3. What's the maximum you can give away, the limit beyond which you will not go?

4. What's the least you can offer without getting laughed out of the room? Here, ruminate over the other party's BATNA, then make sure your worst offer to them is at least some improvement over it.

One final detail before sitting down: Where to conduct the proceedings? John Ilich, author of *The Complete Idiot's Guide*, says preferably on your own home field; failing that, at a neutral location; but never at their place if you can avoid it. Fisher and Bruce Patton, Fisher's co-author for the second edition of *Getting to Yes*, are more flexible. Where would the other party feel most comfortable, if that would serve your purposes? Where are the files, flip charts, white boards, or experts you both will need?

Starting off

You walk in, shake hands, sit down, and you smile. From the first face-to-face contact with the people on the other side, and indeed, in any conversations that may precede the formal negotiation, try to establish as good a person-to-person relationship as possible. You want everybody's energies to go into analyzing the issues and arriving at an imaginative, mutually beneficial solution, not into posturing, bullying, feeling offended, or any other state of high dudgeon that may get in the way of a reasonable outcome.

You can't banish emotions from the proceeding. Rather, the point is to get feelings out into the open, acknowledge them, and, at the least, minimize them as obstacles. At best, you can hope to use them to forge an alliance to speed the work along and, at the end of the negotiation, leave people wanting to do business together again. Without being totally Esalen about it, talk a little about your own feelings, and—carefully—perhaps essay a few words on how the others might be feeling. ("I can imagine that you, too, would like to see a good result from our discussions.") Be polite, respectful, friendly. Show it by not just listening, but hanging on their every word.

To the age-old question, "Do you wait for them to make the first offer, or should you push yours out there first?", Fisher and Patton offer a novel answer: What's the hurry? Putting a number down too soon may foreclose the exploration of interests that both sides should pursue at first. It might even happen that a potential agreement emerges without anybody having to make a "first offer."

If somebody does have to, though, let it be the other guy or gal, advises Ilich. Their first offer immediately sets the upper or lower limit for the negotiation, he argues, the highest you'll have to pay or the lowest you'll be forced to accept.

But why shouldn't you set the limit, other experts retort, particularly since the first offer may well "anchor" the rest of the negotiation, skewing the final result in its direction. In *Negotiating Rationally*, Max H. Bazerman and Margaret A. Neale recount a study they performed asking real estate agents to estimate the right price for a particular house. They divided the realtors into four groups, and gave members of each group packets of information on the house that were identical except for one detail, the price at which the house was supposedly listed for market. Sure enough, the group given the highest listing price set the highest "right price" on it, with the prices estimated by the other groups anchored at successively lower levels by the listing prices provided them.

Setting the anchor yourself works best when the other side hasn't bothered to gather the necessary facts or to think through its interests. To avoid being anchored, counsel Bazerman and Neale, don't make a counter-offer to a ridiculous initial proposal. Better to say, "No thanks; let me know when you're prepared to negotiate seriously."

Moving the Process Along

Much of the emerging wisdom on how to proceed through a negotiation can be distilled into a four-sentence, only semifacetious injunction: To move matters along, ask a question, even in response to a question. If you can't ask a question, fall silent and wait for the other side to step in to end the awkward pause. Only rarely, perhaps to keep up the human side of things, should you make an observation or an assertion. And then immediately tag on a question.

Dig, dig, dig for those interests. Clarify your understanding of what the other side says, this for their edification as well as yours—"How did you arrive at that offer?" Brainstorm together to devise the proverbial "outside the box" solution. Fisher and his colleagues are big proponents of bringing independent, objective standards to bear—benchmarks like market value, costs, past settlements, or scientific judgment—and of using questions to try to get the other side to see the value of such standards. Jandt counters that objectivity flies out the window when the bargaining gets serious.

If both parties are willing to submit to the facts, but can't agree on what the facts are, perhaps a neutral observer can determine both them and the deal they should give rise to. The experts almost all agree that, particularly if you seem headed for an impasse, you should consider submitting your differences to a mediator.

But what if it's only you and them, and they get nasty or tricky? By now you probably can guess the answer—separate the people from the problem, dig for underlying interests, ask a question. A couple of our favorite exemplary responses from *Getting to Yes*, the second edition: "Is there a theory behind having me sit in the low chair with my back to the open door?" And "Shall we alternate spilling coffee on one another day by day?"

Or kick the discussion up one level from a negotiation on the issues to a negotiation on how both sides will negotiate. That is, recognize the other side's gambit for what it is, call it, and suggest getting back to business: "Wow, I haven't seen that classic an example of good cop/bad cop for years. Shall we go back to looking at prices the market has been setting in situations comparable to ours?"

Getting to Finished

As soon as the framework for a possible agreement emerges, ever so gently begin herding the doggies in that direction. Ilich recommends a technique he calls funneling: Remind the other side that this particular issue has been settled, refresh their recollection of what you agreed on, refuse to reopen it, and move on to what's still open.

Especially in a complicated negotiation—say, when there's more than two parties involved—it may help to write down a draft agreement after every major meeting of the minds: "I know we still have a way to go, but I thought I'd set down the terms we appear to have settled on so far? Have I misunderstood anything? What changes would you make?" The mere prospect of having to read the draft over one more time may encourage assent.

Don't hurry them or yourself, Ury counsels. If they feel pressured, they may blow up over a small point. In your haste, you may forget to consult your interests one last time in considering the final terms proposed.

Then, when you think you're in accord at last, ask one more question. Ilich suggests "Have we got a deal?" If they say yes, shake hands, and stop lobbing interrogatories. Should you find yourself at a loss for something to say, talk about the weather.

For Further Reading

The Complete Idiot's Guide to Winning Through Negotiation by John Ilich (1996, Alpha books)

Getting Past No by William Ury (1993, Bantam Books)

Getting to Yes by Roger Fisher and William Ury (1991, Penguin Books)

How to Get What You Want

Do's and Don'ts of
Successful Negotiation

* * *

Imagine the following scenario. A man returns from vacation and goes to the post office determined to collect the mail that has been held for him. But he arrives 10 minutes after the closing bell. He finds a side door that's still open, walks in, and demands to speak to a manager.

The manager decides it's simpler for her to hand over the mail than to argue about it. The man has accomplished the seemingly impossible: getting mail out of a post office after hours.

But what kind of victory was this? The clerks were getting ready to leave, and they all witnessed the man's obnoxious behavior. The next several times he went into the post office, the clerks would mysteriously disappear when they saw him coming. They would put up the "Next Window Please" sign just as he reached the counter.

He treated the negotiation as an attack, and, as a result, he paid for his missteps.

> Ask yourself three questions before preparing for a negotiation: What do you want? Why should they negotiate with you? And what are your alternatives?

How can you improve your chances in the negotiating game? Roger J. Volkema, an expert negotiator and consultant on conflict management and author of *The Negotiation Tool Kit: How to Get Exactly What You Want in Any Business or Personal Situation,* offers some tips.

First of all, he says, understand the golden rule of negotiation: "People will not negotiate with you unless they believe you can help them or hurt them." Your main goal as a negotiator, then, is to understand how you can help or hurt your competition, and how they can help or hurt you.

Volkema advises asking yourself three questions before preparing for a negotiation: What do you want? Why should they negotiate with you? And what are your alternatives?

As for the negotiation itself, Volkema lists some critical do's and don'ts. During the negotiation, ask questions to learn as much as possible about the other party. You can test your understanding through paraphrasing, questioning, and summarizing how the negotiation is progressing. It's good to give out internal information about how the other party's actions are affecting you. And it's good to explain your thinking before you disagree.

But it's counterproductive to go into the defend-and-attack mode as in the post office example. It's ineffective to dilute your position with many arguments; it's better simply to present your two or three strongest reasons. It's very counterproductive to tell the other side what a good deal it is getting; this sort of tactic is called an "irritator" by the experts, and it puts the other side on the defensive.

Volkema divides negotiating styles into three types: the collaborator, the avoider, and the compromiser. The collaborator is most likely to achieve that elusive win-win negotiating success. The avoider will leave many problems unresolved. And the compromiser is likely to get some of what he wants, but not all. It's important to be honest with yourself and to learn which type you are. You may want to create a team of negotiators for important sessions, with the stronger types well represented on the team.

What do you do if someone makes an exaggerated first offer? This is the classic used-car salesman ploy: "How much do you want to pay for the car, guy? One dollar? I'd give it to you free if I could. How much do you want to pay?" Volkema advises either ignoring the offer altogether, or responding with surprise or disbelief.

What do you do if someone delays extensively? Volkema suggests setting the length of the negotiation in advance, and, when that fails, letting the other party know of the point beyond which you will not wait.

The key to successful negotiating, in short, is clarity about your own needs and goals, and a realization that "anything that has been negotiated is negotiable." But that doesn't mean that you should negotiate everything. There are many times when it's simply not worth it. In the final analysis, the man in the example above should have just come back when the post office was open again the following day. The mail can wait.

For Further Reading

The Negotiation Tool Kit: How to Get Exactly What You Want in Any Business or Personal Situation by Roger J. Volkema (1999, AMACOM)

Reprint C0003D

Win-Win with Mark Gordon

The Latest Thinking to Maximize Your
Company's "Return on Negotiation"

* * *

Everyone talks win-win; it's part of the business lexicon. But who is taking care of state-of-the-art negotiating these days, and what is it? We turned to Mark Gordon for answers. Gordon is managing director of CMI/Vantage Partners LLC and senior adviser for the Harvard Negotiation Project at Harvard Law School. As a negotiation specialist, he has advised corporate clients, mediated the settlement of litigation, and facilitated and conducted workshops for executives, union officials, government officials, military officers, and diplomats in the United States, Canada, Europe, Asia, Africa, the

Middle East, and South America. In an interview with writer Royce Flippin, Gordon offers a brief tutorial on win-win and tells us some of the latest thinking on collaborative negotiating.

What's the heart of win-win negotiation?

Gordon: Let me start by saying that I don't use the term "win-win." We prefer terms like collaborative bargaining, joint problem solving, or principled negotiation. For many people, having a paradigm of winning implies a counter-paradigm of losing. I have no qualms about the theory behind win-win—I just don't use that nomenclature.

Could you explain the theory behind it?

Gordon: The theory says that in any interaction it's generally possible to have a "positive sum game"—meaning that negotiating together can produce something good for you and something good for me. This is the converse of the old "zero-sum" negotiation mentality, in which my job is to get you to make concessions. The idea in collaborative bargaining is to negotiate without making concessions to each other, by looking for joint-gain options instead.

Doesn't that go against classical negotiating techniques?

Gordon: Sure—if you read the classic texts, they talk about extreme opening positions, getting the other side to make a concession first, offering to split the difference only after both sides have gone a few rounds, and so on. The collaborative bargaining school says you don't need to make concessions. Instead, you look for creative options. We draw on a fundamental precept from microeconomic theory, which says that in any bilateral negotiation, if there is a range of possible acceptable outcomes, then there is always a set of outcomes that will make both of us happier than the minimum acceptable outcome would.

This implies being prepared to look at many different options.

Gordon: Exactly right. Classical negotiation basically involves trading commitments back and forth. You can play that game without even speaking the same language: when I'm haggling in a bazaar, I can just write down numbers on a piece of paper.

It doesn't work very effectively, though, if I'm trying to negotiate a strategic alliance, or outsource major parts of my nonstrategic business, or develop some other complex business relationship—for the simple reason that it suboptimizes the marketplace, by failing to find all the opportunities for joint gain. You can only do that through a more creative, joint problem-solving model.

How do people get away from the habit of positional thinking?

Gordon: You have to believe that it's in your interest to look for ways to benefit your negotiating counterpart.

Return on Negotiation

The Next Wave in Win-Win Theory

The current cutting-edge thinking doesn't actually concern itself with individual "negotiations" per se. Mark Gordon's consulting firm, CMI/Vantage Partners, prefers instead to use an approach that looks at a company's entire negotiating system—in other words, the whole universe of transactions that take place between that company and other business entities.

"People generally do business with each other for a reason, and that reason usually outlasts any individual transaction," explains Gordon. "For a company to have a sustainable competitive advantage, it has to be able to work in an ongoing, collaborative way with its alliance partners, its suppliers, its customers, and others. In an increasingly interdependent environment, companies have to be able to work with their counterparts in a way that strikes a balance between getting good negotiated outcomes and managing the relationship properly."

CMI/Vantage Partners employs a systematic focus it calls maximizing a company's "return on negotiation," or RON. The aim is to take a company's overall results from its myriad negotiations—which typically follow a bell curve (a few great results, a lot of average results, and a few poor ones)—and shift that curve in a positive direction by revamping the entire negotiating system of the company. Measuring and improving RON offers clear benefits to a company's bottom line without a huge investment up front. "We employ a four-layer model for enhancing an organization's effectiveness," says Gordon. "At the top layer, we're working on skills and behavior. On the second layer, we work on the tools used to enable that behavior—such as negotiating preparation tools, tools for managing conflicts, and tools for measuring how relationships are working. For example, we might help a client do a 'relationship audit,' employing a series of confidential surveys to see how a company's relationships with its partners, suppliers, and customers are doing."

Undergirding all this is a third layer: the systems and structures that support the use of those tools. "People are more likely to use tools that have an impact on the way their performance is judged," notes Gordon. "So we look at incentive structures—both formal incentives (e.g., performance reviews, bonuses, pay raises, promotions)—as well as what's informally rewarded around the workplace (e.g., who gets a pat on the back and a congratulatory note, and for what). Many companies reward salespeople based on their current-period sales, for example—but it's hard to talk about a 'partnership' with your customers if you're rewarding your people only for their short-term sales volume."

Finally, the fourth or "foundation" layer addressed by the Vantage consultants is a corporation's underlying culture and mindset—how that company thinks about itself and its customers, and what sort of attitude it takes toward managing relationships. "If a company has the mindset that it's a dog-eat-dog world out there, and you'd better seize advantage while you can because

> it probably won't be there tomorrow—then providing its employees with joint problem-solving tools won't really accomplish much," observes Gordon.
>
> By improving a company's effectiveness on each of these levels, Vantage hopes to produce an incremental advantage in every negotiation that takes place—creating a substantial improvement in long-term performance.

Your goal is not to hurt them, but to help them at little cost to yourself—and have them help you at little cost to themselves. The more creative you are at coming up with things that are good for both of you, the happier both of you will be.

Is it important for both sides to adopt this approach, or can you use it unilaterally?

Gordon: You can actually use this approach yourself, and entice the other side into playing—because it's a fairly seductive game. If I convince you that my goal is to come up with an agreement that's good for both of us, and that I intend to be flexible and creative in thinking of options that may benefit you but don't hurt me, you're more likely to get drawn into the process. On the other hand, if I play the hard positional game, you're likely to respond with a similar positional hard style, because you know it's going to be a haggling game.

What if we walked through a conflict situation using your model—say a strike?

Gordon: My advice to each side would be the same—first, think hard about what we call your BATNA—best alternative to negotiated agreement—which is what will happen if you can't reach an agreement with the other side. Your BATNA forms the minimum you would accept in a negotiated agreement.... So think hard about the long-term costs and benefits of going to your best alternative. If you're the management side and you don't get an agreement with this union, ask yourself what the impact will be on production, on PR, on your long-term ability to work with the union, on morale, etc. Of course, your goal in a negotiated outcome should be to do substantially better than that, which means you need to understand all of your own interests as well as possible. So you should go on to ask yourself which issues are most important to you: wages, working conditions, environmental issues, benefits. . . .

Once you've identified your own key interests, you should then move on to examine the key interests on the other side. To the extent there are dovetailing interests, those are fruitful grounds to explore. Let's say that both sides want to keep health costs down with maximum benefit for the workers. Instead of fighting over health care dollars, maybe they should design a process for jointly trying to get the cost of health care coverage down. For example, they might appoint a task force from both sides to examine options for changing health care coverage.

In practice, we find that a lot of labor-management teams tend to neglect or gloss over their areas of common interest, and just focus on the areas of conflict—which makes it much harder to resolve their dispute.

How do you implement this approach in an actual negotiation?

Gordon: The first step is to design a process for talking to each other that allows you to brainstorm options jointly without commitment. It's hard to brainstorm if you're afraid you'll be committed to everything that's said, so you need to create a mechanism for talking openly and freely—throwing out ideas and building upon each other's ideas—without fear of premature lock-in to a specific position. So the ground rules are extremely important. Having a facilitator help with this process can be very, very useful.

You'll also want to make sure you have a process for getting through all the issues in a timely fashion. Otherwise, the negotiation deadline can creep up on you, leaving you inadequate time to look for an optimal solution. People often don't start collective-bargaining discussions until very late in the game. We recommend starting preliminary discussions much earlier, so you can begin to invent options before the crunch time comes.

Finally, no matter what we say about creativity, at the end of the day there will be some areas where the interests of both sides conflict to some extent: workers want more money, for example, while management wants to keep costs under control. Some things you can't invent your way around. However, I think the set of interests that is truly conflicting—where it really is a zero-sum game—is usually much smaller than most people think.

Reprint C9903A

A Better Way to Negotiate

Seven Ways to Strengthen Your Business Alliances

* * *

Tom Krattenmaker

The VP of business development—let's call him Jason—was a stickler when it came to contracts. He favored detailed documents that anticipated every conceivable problem and laid out penalties for each. Trust was a foreign concept. In his view, partnerships were built on legalese and the sure promise of reprisals if either party fails to keep up its end of the bargain. So imagine his shock over the proposed contract he encountered in his first meeting with the new partners in Japan; it consisted of two vague paragraphs. Jason was even more befuddled when his Japanese counterparts bristled at his insistence that their simple pact would not do.

Managers are beginning to appreciate the importance of relationships in their companies' dealings with employees, customers, partner companies, and even rivals. Why didn't Jason's company's Japanese partners need a long contract? Because they believed the mutual concern for the relationship would ensure good faith.

"Relationships are a long-neglected aspect of organizations," says Leonard Greenhalgh, a professor at Dartmouth College's Tuck School of Business and the author of *Managing Strategic Relationships: The Key to Business Success.* "Yet when you think about what goes on between individuals, groups, and organizations, management effectiveness depends very much on relationships."

Like Greenhalgh, business author and Cambridge, Mass.-based consultant Chris Turner attributes the new interest in relationships in part to the steady inflow of a new generation of young people who were weaned on the Web and have little interest in contributing their talents to organizations based on hierarchy and regimentation.

"We're definitely in a transition," says Turner, author of *All Hat and No Cattle: Tales of a Corporate Outlaw.* "People are recognizing that command-and-control isn't an effective way to run organizations."

Here are seven concepts experts recommend to managers who want to improve their ability to be more effective in their business relationships.

Recognize That Transactions Are Hardly Ever One-Shot Deals

Jason took pride in his reputation as someone who drove a hard bargain. In his dealings with his company's suppliers, he strove for the bargain-basement price, often pitting supplier against supplier in his quest for the best possible deal. Little did he care that his counterparts usually left with a silent vow to settle the score later. Their opportunity came when Jason's company

> "It is far better to have people regard you with a sense of trust, rapport, and good will than a desire for revenge."

found itself in an emergency and needed to ask for a special favor. Jason got the predictable response: "no." Had Jason and his organization treated the suppliers better—had they fostered a positive relationship—they would have stood a far better chance of finding a cooperative partner when crunch time came.

"Treat people as if you will need to deal with them again," Greenhalgh says. "One-shot deals are very hard to find. It is far better to have people regard you with a sense of trust, rapport, and good will than a desire for revenge."

What about those voluminous contracts? "A comprehensive written contract is necessary only if the relationship is bad," Greenhalgh writes. "It serves as a substitute for trust and good will—but it's not a good substitute. Managers would be better off fixing the relationship."

Negotiate from the Same Side of the Table

Rather than approaching bargaining as a zero-sum contest, one with a winner and a loser, experts suggest putting the negotiators together on the same side of the table, in a figurative sense, united against the challenge or problem.

A competitive man by nature, Jason suffered from what Greenhalgh calls the "fixed-pie syndrome." He couldn't shake the notion that it was his loss every time the other party got something it wanted in the give-and-take. But it is often possible for negotiators to achieve agreements in which both companies end up in a better position than before. For example, if Jason's company agrees to a more generous price for the supplier's widgets, that company might be able to afford manufacturing improvements. Over the long run, Jason's company begins to receive fewer defective parts, and the supplier is better able to help when sudden spikes in demand call for rush orders.

Choose Your Relationships with Care

As your company becomes more mindful of strategic relationships, pay special attention to the people it appoints as representatives. "When you deal with another business, it's not one abstract entity dealing with another abstract entity," Greenhalgh says. "It's one person dealing with another. You need someone who embodies the organization you represent."

According to Turner, the "Vince Lombardi type"—a chest-pumper who calls comrades to arms and sets out to beat the opponent at all costs—is not the person you want representing your organization in the new environment. Nor, says Greenhalgh, will an aggressive person— or someone with a fondness for argument and debate—be effective in forging strategic relationships. The ideal liaisons have a talent for cogent communicating and an ability to achieve and demonstrate understanding of the allies' needs.

Include the Implementers
in the Courting

Too often, says Gene Slowinski, managing partner of Alliance Management Group (Gladstone, N.J.) and director of strategic alliance research at Rutgers' Graduate School of Management, "The deal guy and the lawyer from Company A meet with their counterparts and do a deal. They then throw it over the wall to the implementers and say, 'Don't screw it up.' That's the model that doesn't work." Slowinski recently completed a study in which he learned that successful inter-organization alliances usually involve the "implementers"—the employees who will actually live and work the terms of the agreement—into the deal-making process. This, Slowinski says, can be accomplished by reserving space on both negotiating teams for one or two of the people who will execute the deal.

Including the implementers helps the relationships between organizations, Slowinski says. Because the deal-makers have a realistic grasp of capabilities, expectation errors are eliminated; and because the staffers on the ground are learning about the nascent alliance as it's forming, they're better prepared to begin the execution once the pact is signed.

Foster Cooperation, Not Competition, Between Individuals

According to old-school thinking, the sure way to get the most from your employees is to get them to compete with one another: measure individual performance and award bonuses, raises, and promotions to those who outperform their colleagues. The problem with this approach is that when one employee's gain is another one's loss, people have a powerful disincentive to come together in the kinds of collaborations that will benefit the organization in the long term. The same holds for competition between companies. Rather than going to war with the rival that sells the same service as you, why not work together to grow the sector?

"When you encourage people to excel relative to their peers," Greenhalgh says, "they stop collaborating with one another. If I help someone and she does better as a result, then I'm at risk of losing the competition. Some companies have a rule that you won't be evaluated positively if your success comes at someone else's expense. That's a much better approach."

Another effective approach is to evaluate team, rather than individual, performance. But be careful not to stoke a kind of team-versus-team competition that will plague a company just as surely as when individuals are going at it.

Share the Knowledge

Just like marriages, strategic relationships are built on good communication. Getting too crafty about managing a spouse's information—what to tell and what to keep secret—inevitably leads to a decline in the mutual confidence that the partners can count on one another. The same is true of relationships in your organization, says Turner. "Transparency increases trust, and trust strengthens relationships," she says. "The more information you can get out there the better, because information is power."

Another key to communication is a horizontal, rather than vertical, information flow. In traditional reporting relationships, knowledge travels from top to bottom—from supervisor to manager to worker—and sometimes from bottom to top, as a manager collects intelligence from people on the front lines. But in today's more complex organizations, Greenhalgh says, companies need communication from department to department and team to team. When the information is trapped in vertical "silos," Department A won't benefit from what Department B has just learned about a shift in customer behavior, for example. One effective solution: develop task forces composed of members of different functional areas.

Slowinski urges managers to confront problems with their allies while they're still at the fact level and before they've escalated to the emotional level. At quarterly meetings, he says, time should be reserved to discuss potential problems lest they become full-blown dealwreckers by the next meeting. "Things fester," Slowinski says, "if we don't learn how to bring them up and resolve them."

Create Community, Not Castes

As Greenhalgh reports in his book, managers at the credit card company MBNA have no special section in the parking lot or cafeteria. They dress just like the employees staffing the telephones, and they work out of cubicles like everyone else. The result, Greenhalgh says, is a conspicuous absence of the distance that often grows between managers and employees—a distance that can hurt morale, enthusiasm, and productivity. The MBNA staffers give a spirited effort because all the signals tell them they're valued members of the team.

Turner says there is enormous value in managers' getting to know team members in casual conversation; call it Management by Hanging Around. "One of the most important things a manager can do is get to know the people they're working with," she says. "Part of the work of a leader is to foster the kind of community where good things happen."

Castes, Greenhalgh says, create barriers between people. "This notion of castes is embodied in the practice of referring to the boss as your 'superior,'" he says. "It's implicit in the extra privileges you give to people who are higher up in management. It undermines the effectiveness of the whole institution. If you're doing things that make the caste distinctions more apparent, be prepared for the organization to be less effective as a result."

For Further Reading

All Hat and No Cattle: Tales of a Corporate Outlaw by Chris Turner (2000, Perseus Books)

Managing Strategic Relationships: The Key to Business Success by Leonard Greenhalgh (2001, The Free Press)

Reprint C0105A

Forging and Sustaining Strategic Partnerships

• • •

Companies that make collaborative negotiating a core competency forge positive, mutually beneficial strategic partnerships with other organizations—suppliers, joint-venture partners, newly acquired companies, or even competitors.

The articles in this section explain what to look for in the right strategic partner and how to work out alliance terms that serve both parties' needs and priorities. Several selections also offer suggestions for managers on the other side the strategic-partnership equation: those whose companies have been approached by another organization to form an alliance. To be selected as a strategic partner, you need to submit a well-crafted proposal and frame the outcomes of the deal in positive terms.

Once an alliance has been forged, both parties must work to manage the relationship day to day. When both organizations have embedded collaborative bargaining in their managerial systems, sustaining strategic partnerships becomes easier.

How to Negotiate an Alliance You Can Live With

* * *

Rebecca M. Saunders

Strategic alliances dominate today's business landscape. Some company is always announcing agreements with its supply chain partners, competitors—even former customers. Is an alliance right for your company? Begin by figuring out what you could gain from a partnership and what assets you could provide in return. Follow up with a negotiation strategy that will make the deal work for all parties.

Getting Started

Know What You Want to Achieve

You need to be clear about your firm's objectives at every step of the process. Roger J. Volkema, author of *The Negotiation Tool Kit,* advises, "Write your objectives down and then prioritize them. Identify deal breakers. That way, during negotiations, when it comes to making concessions, the team will know how far it can bend." A key point, Volkema stresses, is to "create the list as a group to ensure that everyone on the team is on the same page." Brainstorming can be an effective way to build that list.

Court Your Prospective Partner

"Courtship is a good term to use for this initial phase since your ultimate goal is to build a relationship," says Dr. Mitchell Lee Marks, coauthor (with Philip H. Mirvis) of *Joining Forces.* The point of this courtship phase is to eliminate unsuitable partners, so you will need to study prospective candidates' annual reports, press clippings, and public relations. Talk to their customers, too. If possible, attend industry meetings at which their executives will speak to determine long-term corporate plans. "You want to find a company whose goals align with yours," says Marks, whether the company is in the same industry as yours or not.

Be Up Front

Alert prospective partners about your interest in an alliance, says Mimi Donaldson, coauthor (with Michael C. Donaldson) of *Negotiating for Dummies.* Don't keep your purpose to yourself until you have felt them out. "Let your counterpart know why you want to meet." But, she adds, "keep quiet on the details of the proposed partnership until you are in the same room. This will enable the prospective partner to bring colleagues critical to such discussions to the first meeting yet ensure your specific plans are kept proprietary until you know there is interest in the deal." Later in negotiations, you may have to bring in a lawyer to prepare a confidentiality agreement, but early discussions generally should be broad enough to allow free speech.

Coming to Terms

Congratulations—you've identified the ideal business partnership from a field of possibilities, courted the lucky organization, and convinced it to join forces with you. But that was the easy part. Now it's time to negotiate terms—and that's where most alliances are won or lost. The key to success is knowing how to identify a shared vision and common goals. Here's how savvy dealmakers do it:

Build a Team That Can Pull in One Direction

Those with whom you negotiate should have the power to make decisions and to understand the management implications of any issues on the table. The same goes for members of your own team. Donaldson knows from her 20 years' experience counseling managers on their negotiating style that personality conflicts crop up frequently in negotiations. "You might find yourself dealing with someone who is cantankerous or whose personal communication style might slow discussions. But you shouldn't let these issues tempt you to exclude the individual from your group." The only factor that should influence someone's place on the team, according to Donaldson, is his or her support for the team mission. "Everyone on your team should be on board as far as goals are concerned, even if only in a passive way," she says.

Begin Negotiations by Clearly Stating Mutual Goals or Needs

Each team should state clearly its needs or objectives for such an alliance. Honesty is critical, says Volkema. Don't hold back or distort your needs. Nor should you use this opportunity to take an inflexible position. "Your goal is to unveil your true interests," says Yves L. Doz, Timken Chaired Professor of Global Technology and Innovation at INSEAD, France, and coauthor (with Gary Hamel) of *Alliance Advantage*.

Share Information Willingly

In labor or vendor negotiations, information is often seen as power to be hoarded. Not so in strategic negotiations. "In traditional negotiations," says Doz, "collaboration begins at the end of negotiation. In alliance negotiations, such collaborations must be part of the process from the start." Doz continues, "Expectations and commitments should be stated openly and clearly." On the other hand, the total scope of potential benefits to your firm—that is, the indirect value of the alliance or partnership to your firm—need not be discussed.

> The key to successful negotiation is knowing how to identify a shared vision and common goals.

Promote Trust

One or another of the parties has to start by showing a willingness to be straightforward and open. It might as well be you, says Donaldson. "Where trust among negotiators is missing," she says, "one or the other party winds up a loser, and the relationship between the two remains antagonistic even if a partnership is solidified." That negativity will hinder the partnership's success for all involved.

Listen, Listen, Listen

You want to verify your assumptions, says Marks. The sooner you understand your partner's needs, the sooner you will identify points of commonality and differences. Then you can explore options that would satisfy everyone.

Abandon Unrealistic Expectations

If you have done sufficient homework, you know what will be acceptable conditions to the other party and what clearly won't. So, says Volkema, don't come to the initial meeting with ideas that you know will be rejected by the other party. Still, your research should have identified telling arguments for an alliance or a partnership, and you may want to use these during your talks.

Don't Look upon the Other Company's Team as "The Enemy"

As Doz warns, you shouldn't think of yourselves as opponents during discussions. "It's an attitude that can carry over to the detriment of actual management of the partnership if the negotiations are successful. Your goal should be mutual gain; the outcome must call for either mutual gain or a stalemate so neither party loses."

Bring Untouchable Issues to the Table

You know what issues you can't bend on. Let the prospective partner's team know these. Says Donaldson, "Be up front. Encourage the same from the other firm. Too frequently, parties to the negotiation hide their sacred cows. Consequently, after the agreement is struck, both parties find themselves with a herd of cows they can't support."

Let Feelings Out

Marks observes that partnership discussions can raise issues that trigger emotional responses, like fear that jobs will be lost or career aspirations thwarted. Such emotional responses should be aired. They are more likely to create outbursts when an effort is made to ignore them than when they are addressed.

Don't Rush

It takes time to reach an agreement that will enable you and your new partner to work well together—particularly if you are corporate competitors. Doz suggests that as negotiations move forward, you should include in the meeting those people who will "have to live with the consequences of whatever agreement is reached; i.e., the implementers who will be in charge of the alliance. Also include others, like finance types to provide safeguards and, if needed, a good cop–bad cop position." Involving this many people will add significantly to negotiation time; be prepared for that.

Raise Questions

You've done your research, but it may not have been sufficient to understand fully your partner's viewpoint; you need to separate the reality from assumptions made based on limited knowledge acquired. The questions asked should fill the gaps in information and clarify muddy issues, says Volkema. Don't use questions to make points that position you as winner and the other party as loser in the negotiations. Don't just ask questions, either—be ready to answer them.

Summarize Periodically

As the negotiation moves to its conclusion, says Donaldson, one team leader should summarize points of agreement. Not only does this ensure that all are seeing what is transpiring in the same light but also it creates an upbeat atmosphere, as one point of contention after another is resolved to everyone's satisfaction.

In the strange world of modern business alliances, your competitor today may be your partner tomorrow—

and your competitor again the day after tomorrow. Conduct these negotiations with care, openness, and one eye on the future.

For Further Reading

Alliance Advantage: The Art of Creating Value through Partnering by Yves L. Doz and Gary Hamel (1998, Harvard Business School Press)

Joining Forces: Making One Plus One Equal Three in Mergers, Acquisitions, and Alliances by Mitchell Lee Marks, Ph.D. and Philip H. Mirvis (1998, Jossey Bass)

Negotiating for Dummies by Michael C. Donaldson and Mimi Donaldson (1996, Hungry Minds, Inc.)

The Negotiation Tool Kit: How to Get Exactly What You Want in Any Business or Personal Situation by Roger J. Volkema (1999, AMACOM)

Reprint C0104B

Making Your Proposal Come Out on Top

• • •

Nick Wreden

Nancy Sucher doesn't just read proposals. She looks for the start of a relationship—a partner who recognizes her needs and will speak to her clearly.

To Sucher, procurement negotiation manager at the $3.5 billion Boise Office Solutions, an office supplies and paper distributor in Itasca, Ill., potential relationships start from following the RFP (Request for Proposal) instructions precisely. Not only do proposals that follow a different organization create more work for

Sucher and her staff, they also raise a red flag. "If they don't listen to us—the customer—now, will they listen to us later?" she asks.

Selling may woo prospects, but customers are often won with proposals. Done right, proposals can be your best avenue to new business, funding, or opportunities. Done wrong, they are a waste of time and money. The key to increasing your winning percentage is bearing in mind the prospect's needs at all levels of the process. This rule applies as much to meeting the basic specs of the submission as it does to how skillfully you assess and respond to the prospect's needs. Ideally, this approach results in a concise, readable, and persuasive document.

Work from the Prospect's Point of View

Understand that while companies use proposals to underscore why they should be chosen, prospects, who face a pile of five, ten, or even more proposals, are actually seeking reasons to eliminate candidates. "Companies don't start by looking to select the best proposal. They seek to eliminate all those that don't meet their criteria. That means it's critical to make it as hard as possible to be eliminated during the initial review," says Dan Safford, CEO of the Seattle-based proposal-writing and training firm PS Associates. Let the prospect's requirements drive the process. Proposals should never be about what you can do, but what you can do for prospects. "A good proposal specifically addresses a prospect's needs," says Michael Kelley, a PricewaterhouseCoopers partner who specializes in global advertising, branding, and marketing. "A poor proposal discusses only your credentials." Never, for example, start a proposal by describing your corporate history.

Follow a Disciplined Process

A systematic, repeatable proposal process ensures that all requirements—and proposal budgets—are met. It reduces the last-minute rush that breeds ineffectiveness and errors. It contributes to accurate pricing so that the job is both winnable and profitable.

Following the right process can help avoid elimination. If you're responding to an RFP, follow its instructions to the letter. Sucher, for example, requires proposals to be unbound to speed copying and review. If the presentation requirements are not spelled out, call the prospect to determine the expected format.

Reinforce this with a prospect meeting whenever possible. Kelley says such meetings clarify the RFP, provide insights about the selection criteria and decision makers, and start establishing the relationships that can lead toward selection.

This process includes:

Thorough Research

"Spend at least as much time in studying, analyzing, planning, researching, and otherwise preparing to write as in writing itself," writes Herman Holtz in *The Consultant's Guide to Proposal Writing*. Research, backed by a clear understanding of prospect requirements, enables you to develop strategies, solutions, staffing requirements, and even pricing. Often it's helpful to show prospects initial efforts in these areas and ask for feedback, says Kelley. Such guidance can help ensure that your efforts fulfill expectations.

Timetables and an Outline of Responsibilities

You'll need to determine timetables, responsibilities, and budgeting. Schedule responsibilities for key personnel, including managers, writers, and technical experts. Include time for multiple drafts, graphics development, reviews, and production activities such as copying and binding.

Careful Attention to Writing

The most vital part of the process is, of course, writing. The proposal must clearly document an understanding of the problem, explain a solution, describe activities, and detail anticipated results. "Proposals are often won or lost on the effectiveness of the writing," says G. Jay Christensen, who specializes in teaching business communications at California State University in Northridge, Calif. "Use simple, conversational English, with one idea per sentence. Avoid jargon. Revise, and revise again, for clarity." Back up claims with case studies, research, or third-party recognition.

Organize the Framework

A key element of the proposal is the executive summary. Executive summaries are like movie trailers. They pique interest with appealing highlights, communicate the essence of the coming presentation, and help the audience determine whether to invest further time and information.

As a result, an executive summary demands your best thinking—and writing. Often, it is the only section read by decision makers. Within limited space, the executive summary must communicate key analyses, capabilities, and benefits persuasively enough to compel the reader to read the entire proposal. No wonder Safford calls an executive summary "an elevator speech in print."

"But despite their importance, most people do not devote enough time to executive summaries," says Christensen. "Executive summaries don't write themselves. They require an in-depth understanding of the proposal as well as an ability to succinctly communicate reader-specific benefits with punch and verve."

Executive summaries are neither prefaces nor introductions. They are not the place to introduce new material. Crucial elements of an executive summary include analysis, scope, recommendations, implementation highlights, and, most important, benefits. Length can range from one or two paragraphs to one or two pages. One rule of thumb says an executive summary should be 10% to 15% of the length of the proposal.

However, like proposals, the more concise executive summaries are, the better. Use bullet points to telegraph prime concepts or activities. Avoid fluff like "We are pleased to present. . . ." Instead, point out that you propose setting up a European distribution network that can increase sales 40% by 2005. Says Kelley: "The more specific it is, the more they'll know you've listened and understand their problems." Don't be afraid to mention pricing; prospects will immediately scan the proposal for it anyway.

Experts debate about whether to write the executive summary before or after the proposal. Writing it beforehand establishes the framework and themes for the proposal. It also avoids the common trap of having the executive summary masquerade as a conclusion. Writing the executive summary afterward simplifies the capture of relevant points, primarily by culling key sentences. Consider combining the strengths of both approaches. Write an executive summary beforehand to crystallize themes and benefits, then revise that summary in the context of the final proposal.

Regardless of when you write the executive summary, start with a one-sentence summary that encapsulates the prospect's problem, your solution, and the benefits. Expand that sentence into about 100 words. Then add supporting points until the most important issues have been summarized.

Another valuable tool is the response matrix, a three- or four-column spreadsheet that outlines the specification, indicates compliance or another response, and shows where the requirement is addressed in the proposal. It can include a blank column for notes or check-off. The response matrix is excellent for indicating where you have addressed important issues not specifically raised in the RFP. Providing summaries in the margins, as a college textbook does, also speeds comprehension and review.

The appendix, in turn, is an opportunity to expand or document points made in the main body. This material can range from brochures to photographs to even video. PricewaterhouseCoopers sometimes includes a CD-ROM with an organizational chart featuring members of the proposed team. Prospects can click on the name of a specific manager and see both a tailored résumé and a short personal introduction on video.

Other key tips for creating winning proposals include

Personalize, Personalize, Personalize

Proposals must be presented from the prospect's point of view. Emphasize specific benefits and value over your general capabilities and expertise. Edit standard résumés to reflect experience important to the prospect. Pricewater-houseCoopers even emphasizes aspects of its corporate history according to the needs of specific prospects.

Avoid boilerplate, despite its value as a timesaver. Boilerplate language in proposals is like junk mail in a mailbox—easy to spot and an easy excuse to discard the proposal. It also sends the message that you do not consider the project important enough for personalization. The only acceptable boilerplate is standard contracts, rate sheets, and proprietary and nondisclosure statements.

Remember That Details Sell

Avoid generalities and hyperbole. Banish every "uniquely qualified," "extensive experience," and other vague braggadocio that undermines credibility. Instead of saying, "We will provide a useful manual," explain that a 50-page, $6'' \times 9''$ booklet will have an operational checklist as well as 10 questions at the end of every section to ensure understanding. Even avoid generic labels like "proposal." Instead, use a description like "a comprehensive program to improve quality through cost-effective inventory management."

Paint a Picture

Graphics communicate clearly and are particularly useful for explaining complex processes. Tables with features and benefits are especially powerful. Also use graphic elements such as call-out boxes to highlight key points. Summarize with bullets where appropriate.

Be Concise

Keep the proposal as short as possible. Some RFPs have page limits; make that an outer limit, not a target. It's tempting to add everything that a prospect might be remotely interested in, but such material dilutes your ideas and capabilities. One distinct benefit: short proposals usually get read first, which makes yours the standard by which others are judged.

Take Time to Assess

The proposal process doesn't end after submission. Proposals that have survived the prospect's best elimination efforts can generate an invitation to present. The prospect uses this opportunity not only to address issues raised in the proposal but also to determine chemistry and competence.

Win or lose, ask for a debriefing. Debriefings are vital for improving the proposal management process and bolstering your win-loss record. If you win, find out why. Which areas stood out, and which were ignored? "Client guidance after the contract is awarded can also help you execute the project more successfully," says Safford. Sometimes, clients may even be willing to turn over losing proposals for additional insights.

Loss debriefings are also valuable. Finding out why you were eliminated can strengthen future proposals. On occasion, it can provide a springboard to further work, especially if your recommendations or skills in a particular area were strong. "Both win and loss debriefings give me the opportunity to build a longer-term relationship, which is my prime objective," says Kelley.

Too often, proposals are marketing afterthoughts, left to the last minute and filled with search-and-replace generalities. No wonder success rates suffer, and proposals get associated with uncertain return from extended effort. But well-written proposals can actually be your best sales tool—and the start of a long relationship.

For Further Reading

The Consultant's Guide to Proposal Writing: How to Satisfy Your Clients and Double Your Income by Herman Holtz (1998, John Wiley & Sons)

Reprint C0207A

The Right Frame

Managing Meaning and
Making Proposals

. . .

Marjorie Corman Aaron

You are intent on persuading senior management to let your division buy a small business with complementary products. You think capturing these products and their brand name is critical to the division's future growth. However, the purchase will involve either a significant cash outlay or a lot more debt, just when the company is expanding in other directions as well. You're convinced the acquisition would be wise. How can you maximize the chances of a "yes" from management? Should your presentation frame the decision as a "risk worth taking" or an "opportunity we can't afford to miss"?

The fact is, how you frame the proposal will have a big effect on what happens to it. Why so? Because framing affects the way we understand the proposal. "Just like a photographer, when we select a frame... we choose which aspect or portion of the subject we will focus on and which we will exclude," observe Gail T. Fairhurst and Robert A. Sarr in *The Art of Framing: Managing the Language of Leadership*. "When we choose to highlight some aspect, we make it more noticeable, more meaningful and more memorable." The authors further note that framing "adds color or accentuates the subject.... Frames determine whether people notice problems, how they understand and remember problems, and how they evaluate and act on them." Frames either focus or obscure; they have the power both to influence and to distort.

How can you capture the power of framing when making a proposal or launching a corporate change initiative?

Effective framing taps in to mental models

We each carry mental models of how to behave under various conditions, and framing may determine the mental model we decide to follow. Say a bank officer faces demands to redress the impact of the bank's lending policies on local community groups. He could frame the demands to the board of directors as a "shakedown," thereby invoking a mental model that resists "knuckling under to pressure." But if he framed it as a business problem—the need to earn the good will of the community—the board might be persuaded to fund some programs. If he framed the bank's circumstances as "wrestling with a 500-pound gorilla," the board would probably do whatever it would take to get the gorilla off its back, and quickly.

Here's another example. Imagine that you are a VP of a small engineering firm negotiating with a large general contractor regarding cost overruns. He's intent on discussing every dime. Instead, you might refer to the larger frame—the multimillion-dollar magnitude of the overall project—and note the savings your work generated in other areas. Or, you might mention his company's size (in comparison to yours) as a reason that it doesn't make sense for him to "sweat the small stuff."

Metaphors are powerful; use them with care

As illustrated by the 500-pound gorilla, metaphor helps us understand and experience one thing in terms of another and leads us to apply the rules and values it suggests. A CEO proposing a joint venture may frame the opportunity by using the metaphor of "a train leaving the station." To fail to jump on board is to be left behind. A manager opposing the venture may frame it as "hopping on the bandwagon," highlighting the foolishness of joining without the benefit of careful analysis. In each case, the metaphor pushes us to focus on a different aspect of the issue at hand.

Using metaphor to frame a management plan can help achieve implementation. When the manager of a power plant explained the three elements of his public affairs program during an environmental cleanup effort, he compared the program to a "three-legged stool." This metaphor dramatized the need for all three legs to support the public's perception. The metaphor is powerful because of its "entailments"—the relationships and concepts it evokes, which are analogous and persuasive.

However, a metaphor's entailments can be dangerous. Fairhurst and Sarr describe how a company president's speech to employees backfired because of conflicting and negative entailments. The president first used the metaphor of the company as family. But, when he went on to introduce some change initiatives, he referred to the "train leaving. . . . You had better not be the last ones on the train or you will find your seat taken." The entailments of abandonment and threats made the family metaphor ridiculous. Don't mix your metaphors when the stakes are high.

Use psychology to frame your proposals better

People are psychologically hardwired to prefer or avoid certain choices, say psychologists Daniel Kahneman and Amos Tversky, who described a model of rational decision making—prospect theory—that maps the value of the various outcomes as a function of gains and losses. Their research demonstrated that positive and negative framing has a significant effect on how people make decisions. If you frame a proposal to exploit this psychological hardwiring, you are more likely to elicit the response you seek.

To encourage acceptance of a compromise proposal, for example, avoid framing it as "[only so much] less than your original demand." Instead, frame it positively, as "[so much] more than the initial offer," and as "funds that would be yours now." Making the proposal tangible strengthens the strategy: you might bring a check and a draft compromise agreement. In this way, the deal becomes tangible—the certain gain—and to reject it is to lose what was literally "on the table."

Frame with risk preferences and aversions in mind

Kahneman and Tversky's research shows that people would rather risk potentially larger future losses than face certain losses now. This preference comes into play when you negotiate to settle a legal business dispute. Even if a defendant understands that he faces the risk of a large verdict against him, he may find it more difficult to settle and pay now. Similarly, a plaintiff may take a smaller settlement because he doesn't want to risk losing what is on the table.

Encourage joint risk taking
by negative framing

Negative framing can be very effective, too, under the right circumstances. Say your division wants a special allocation of marketing funds for a new product. Sales so far have been disappointing because of some glitches in the product (now corrected) and misjudgment of the target market. You might frame the proposal to the marketing manager by saying: "To pull the plug now would be to write off all the marketing effort that has gone into this so far. Without your help, the product will be a dismal failure." This frame also plays upon the common psychological tendencies to commit and to avoid regret. People hold positive illusions about the quality of their decisions. If the marketing manager refuses the allocation, she may face regret over the initial marketing strategy and resource allocation. Agreeing to a second try allows her to avoid regret as she takes a risk with your product.

To win approval of a change proposal,
de-emphasize commitment
and responsibility

Research has shown that people often remain committed to a course of action long after evidence or changed circumstances makes it unwise, particularly if they were

How to Clinch the Deal Using a Positive Frame

Let's say a popular apparel company is trying to sign an exclusive contract with an Olympic gold medalist. Each side of the negotiation will be affected by the way the questions are framed. The athlete may think, What could I lose by signing this exclusivity deal? What could I gain by joining this venture as an exclusive agent? The apparel company's management may be thinking, What will we gain by capturing this sports hero? What can the business lose by tying up capital and linking its marketing efforts to the uncertainties of athletic competition?

A negotiation experiment by Max Bazerman, visiting professor at Harvard Business School, and Margaret Neale of the Stanford Graduate School of Business illustrates the impact of positive or negative framing—framing as gain or loss—on negotiation decisions.

largely responsible for that original course. For example, experienced mountain climbers can get trapped by decisions to scale the summit, and thus fail to turn back in dangerous weather. A sizable business investment becomes a sunk cost and too often drives managers to throw good money after bad. The more directly responsible the manager is for the original investment decision, the more difficult it will be for him to retreat.

How can you change this kind of thinking? Say you are championing a proposal to radically change your

When they *positively* framed the goal of a collective bargaining experiment as achieving a *gain*—telling negotiators that any agreement better than the current contract represented gain to their constituents—more negotiators reached agreements and viewed the outcomes as fair.

In contrast, when a negative frame was used—telling negotiators that any concessions made from the initial offers represented losses to their constituents—fewer negotiators made concessions or reached agreements, and they were less likely to view the outcomes as fair. In a similar business-contract negotiation experiment, framing the goal as maximizing profits or minimizing expenses yielded parallel results. Thus, the apparel company should frame the deal with the athlete as a positive opportunity for growth with the brand. And the athlete should stress the positive ways in which the sports connection will broaden the company's reach and appeal.

division's marketing approach. You can override the commitment to the current marketing plan by framing the decision as an entirely new one. Emphasize recent demographic changes, newer user profiles, and the changes in the ways consumers obtain information: "We have an opportunity here to reach the Gen X market—we need to set up a highly interactive Web site to reel them in." Create face-saving distance between the decision-makers and the past, to make it less painful for them to accept change.

Frame to exploit or undermine endowment

Ownership changes the way we value things. Once we feel ownership, we often put a higher value on an item than we would be willing to pay for it. Stanford University psychologists describe a series of experiments in which subjects given a mug valued it at a much higher average price than did those given money and permission to buy the mug, or those allowed to choose between the mug or money. Most people selling a house or a business will experience a much deeper sense of this kind of endowment.

How can you frame to avoid or exploit this effect? Experienced salespeople seek to create endowment, referring to whatever they are selling as "yours." When purchasing from a longtime owner, however, the endowment effect can be an obstacle. The buyer might frame his proposal not as "selling the home you've lived in all your life," but rather as "offering the opportunity to achieve your retirement objectives." Skilled negotiators try to create parallel endowment in the negotiation process itself, so that completion of the deal becomes another source of value.

One sum—or multiple parts?

Research indicates that people value a series of small gains more than a single gain of the same amount. However, people are less upset by one large loss than by an identical loss suffered in multiple parts. When framing a proposal to a buyer, a seller-negotiator might describe the merits of each package component separately, but speak of the total cost: "When you hire our computer consulting firm, you'll get all the necessary cabling, a fully networked system, and 25 hours of tech support for one low price." However, when framing the same deal proposal to the seller, a buyer-negotiator might state separately the price for each component: "We'll pay you X amount for the cabling, Y amount for the system, and Z amount for the support."

Framing is the active management of meaning, which affects your listeners' understanding of and reaction to the intended message. Business managers are well advised to frame messages strategically, mindful of the potential force of metaphor and human psychology.

For Further Reading

The Art of Framing: Managing the Language of Leadership by Gail T. Fairhurst and Robert A. Sarr (1996, Jossey-Bass, Inc.)

Judgment in Managerial Decision Making by Max H. Bazerman (1998, John Wiley & Sons, Inc.)

Metaphors We Live By by George Lakoff and Mark Johnson (1983, University of Chicago Press)

Negotiating Rationally by Max H. Bazerman and Margaret A. Neale (1993, The Free Press)

Reprint C9909A

After the Deal Is Done

Four Keys to Managing an Alliance

• • •

Stephen Bernhut

Few phrases capture the hubris and hell-bent-for-growth attitude of the 1990s like "done deal." And perhaps nowhere was the phrase used more frequently as an exclamation point than for the thousands of strategic alliances formed in those bubble years.

An alliance is an agreement between two or more partners to make certain decisions—for example, marketing or distribution decisions—jointly. It's not a merger or an acquisition; no new entity is created. Much like the sudden deflation of the dot-com bubble, many of the done-deal alliances of recent years are fast coming undone. "Alliance management today is in crisis," says Jeff Weiss, of Vantage Partners, a Cambridge, Mass., consulting firm that specializes in alliances and recently published a three-year study of alliance practices. "More and more alliances are being formed, yet there is still a very high rate of failure."

The Vantage study found that of the 70% of alliances that fail, poor day-to-day management of the alliance relationship is the cause of breakdown in 64% of the cases. In the space of a few years, the focus has shifted from the deal itself to managing the deal. "An alliance today is increasingly viewed as a strategic relationship, and its success is predicated on implementing and sustaining a systematic approach to managing the relationship day to day," says Weiss. "Although there are very clear best practices for managing an alliance, most companies don't take managing an alliance seriously."

Many alliance partners seem to believe that an invisible hand will steer its alliance in the right direction. "To make these relationships work you need to be very systematic, to develop a strategic map, a well-thought-out communications plan, even plans about how often you will meet," says Anton Gueth, a director in Eli Lilly's office of alliance management (Indianapolis).

The breakup of the eight-year-old alliance between Hewlett-Packard (Palo Alto, Calif.) and Dell Computer (Austin, Tex.) has caused some to wonder whether alliances are falling out of favor. "I wouldn't generalize from the HP-Dell breakup," says Benjamin Gomes-Casseres, a professor of international business at Brandeis University (Waltham, Mass.). "It's always been true that alliances between rivals are not likely to work out."

The conditions of the HP-Dell alliance changed as Dell entered HP's printing markets. "If this means that companies will now become more hesitant about forming an alliance with a competitor, then that is all for the better. Many have entered alliances with blinders on, claiming not to see any conflict. But the result is not necessarily that fewer alliances will be formed." Here again, Dell proves the example: as it expands into the storage-systems market, Dell has recently entered into an alliance with EMC (Hopkinton, Mass.).

> With the failure of M&As, alliances have become the vehicle of choice for growth.

Adds Peter Pekar, the national director of alliances for investment bank Houlihan Lokey Howard and Zukin (Washington, D.C.): "There's no question at all that corporations will continue to choose to bond rather than build or buy to stimulate growth and increase corporate wealth." One of the main reasons for this: with the failure of M&As, alliances have become the vehicle of choice for growth—this despite the management problems many alliances are experiencing.

Just what are the building blocks of a successful alliance? The following four practices share the recognition that an alliance is a long-term relationship, and one that begins only after the deal is done.

1: Make Alliance Management a Core Capability

Perhaps the most glaring shortcoming among companies today is their failure to institutionalize the best practices that constitute successful alliance management. "Companies that institutionalize an alliance capability have an 80% success rate, versus only 10% for those that do not," says Pekar. "What's more, their return on investment is 100% higher."

One of the most comprehensive—and successful—programs for managing alliances is outlined in Hewlett-Packard's 200-page alliance management guide. "It encapsulates 10 years of experience and learning," says Jason Wakeam, HP's director of operations for global alliances. "It has 40 different tools for managing an alliance, including an eight-step methodology that guides a manager through the life cycle of an alliance."

Another option, says Pekar, is to build a "center of excellence," where managers "can learn about contracts, audits, and best practices. Many companies won't form an alliance with a firm that doesn't have such a center because "they will spend too much time training personnel."

2: Build and Manage Trust

To make an alliance work, employees must be able to transcend their own company's interests and work for the broader good of the alliance. "The real game is to grow the whole pie, not to slice it up so your company can get a bigger piece," says Douglas Reid, an assistant professor of strategy at Queen's University in Kingston, Ontario. "You do that by trusting the people in your alliance. And the only way you do that is by realizing that trust is built by and between people, not organizations." To establish a proper foundation for a trusting, genuinely collaborative relationship:

- Make sure that some of the people negotiating the alliance will also be managing it. "Companies that do well," says Reid, "try not to have hand-offs from negotiators to managers. Every time you have a hand-off, you deplete the amount of social capital. Every time you delegate, that person starts at zero. They have no sense of the other organization at all."

- Keep the commitments you make, whether it's a meeting date or a responsibility to deposit funds. "Any deviation from a pattern or an agreed-upon routine will be interpreted as breaking the faith with the collective culture of the alliance," says Reid. "Inconsistency could promote distrust."

- Know your partner's goals. "Trust sometimes breaks down because of inadvertence, not malice," says Reid. "Finding out what matters to your partner eliminates friction caused by trying to interpret their actions." Adds Lilly's Gueth: "It's harder to demonize the other side if you know them personally."

- Build consensus. As you address specific issues, it's important not to jump to a solution. "That just polarizes people," says David Straus, author of *How to Make Collaboration Work* (Berrett-Koehler, 2002). Instead, build consensus step by step. "Back up and get agreement on the definition and analysis of the issue."

3: Audit the Relationship

"Despite the ubiquity of alliances, few companies systematically track their performance . . . leading many alliances to be run by intuition and incomplete information," write McKinsey consultants James Bamford and David Ernst ("Managing the Alliance Portfolio," *The McKinsey Quarterly,* No. 3, 2002).

But even measuring business and technical milestones is not enough. "Measuring the emotional health of an alliance is as, or even more important than, evaluating technical factors," says Gueth. Which is why it's helpful to designate a relationship manager who'll be responsible for tending to the alliance itself, not just the business issues.

One of the audits Lilly uses to evaluate its alliances is called "The Voice of the Alliance." Once a year, a third-party firm sends a Web-based survey of 70 questions to alliance personnel in both companies. The questions focus on 14 strategic operating and cultural dimensions that Lilly has identified as the keys to alliance success— for example, communication, conflict management, and organizational values.

"The results have led to some very important and positive changes," says Gueth. "At times we've changed people because the chemistry wasn't right, and at other times we've changed the structure and reporting processes of certain committees."

4: Develop a Protocol for Joint Decision Making

"Joint decision making is the soul of every alliance. It's also the raison d'être, so it must be done right," says Brandeis's Gomes-Casseres. Like managing sudden change, joint decision making is much less onerous when you use a template that captures the key elements. *Mastering Alliance Strategy,* coauthored by Gomes-Casseres, describes one such protocol.

Among its most critical steps:

- Create a task force—before the deal is finalized—consisting of two to four executives from different operating areas and from each partner.

- List the 20–50 most significant decisions that need to be made, sort them into categories, and rank them by importance.

- Identify the key stakeholders in the key decisions. Encourage "shadow" decision makers who can make or block a decision to identify themselves.

- Develop a spectrum that will show the role that each decision maker should play in making a particular decision: commit, negotiate, consult, notify, or delegate.

- Draw a decision path, a graphic representation of the trajectory and individuals involved in making the necessary decisions. This helps ward off the anxiety that can develop when people can't see what's ahead.

Implementing these best practices will do more than enable an organization to manage an alliance effectively.

"Once growth returns, alliances will prove to be a great vehicle for finding solutions that are not so obvious," says HP Canada's Geoff Kereluik.

Reprint U0212D

Negotiation as a Business Process

. . .

Jeff Weiss

Negotiations are no longer predictable but infrequent events that can be handled by a few professionals. The rise of strategic sourcing and integrated sales, and companies' increased reliance on acquisitions and alliances, have made negotiations more complex, dynamic, and more critical. With all these changes comes the opportunity to create a new organizational capability. The individual elements of a negotiation are well known. By taking a strategic and systematic approach to them all— not just the time spent across the table from the other side's negotiators, but the preparation and review phases as well—companies can turn negotiation into a business process replete with tools for creating value out of each activity.

Phase I: Gaining and Sustaining Internal Alignment

A few simple steps can prevent negotiating teams from picking up mixed messages. For example, for each negotiation it undertakes, the sales division of a large manufacturer identifies the key decisions senior managers must make; which managers should be involved in which decisions, and to what extent; and the process by which each key decision will be made.

Phase II: Providing Instructions

It's not enough to tell the negotiating team, "Don't bring back any less than that." Negotiators need more nuanced guidance—and rigorous measures of success. Instead of telling a negotiating team simply to acquire a certain compound made by biotech firm A for as little money as possible, it's vastly more helpful to tell the team that a successful negotiated outcome with firm A involves minimizing time to market and managing risk, even at the expense of larger investments up front, and that any deal will need to be measured up against two alternative deals with firms B and C. The business development group of a pharmaceutical company has developed instruction templates that require the managers to provide instructions to the negotiating team to spell out the following: the key interests that need to be satisfied; the criteria by which the negotiators should evaluate possible solutions; "walkaways," best alternatives to a negotiated agreement; and goals for the kind of working relationship that should be forged during the negotiations.

Phase III: Preparing for the Negotiation

Instead of leaving negotiators to find their own way, many firms are adopting standard methods and tools for negotiation preparation. One example is the procurement division of a major entertainment company. To help teams of negotiators prepare together, the division created an intranet site complete with templates for organizing the teams, analytical tools for better understanding the other side and assessing its negotiating context, databases of effective terms and persuasive standards, and planning tools for generating creative solutions and choosing among the various options. The previously mentioned business development group has initiated a "negotiation launch" that focuses on how the deal will be negotiated. This daylong, structured event helps all the parties in the negotiation determine the ground rules for the process and decide how predictable stumbling blocks will be managed.

Phase IV: Conducting the Negotiations

Even the way negotiations are handled once the parties have sat down together can be improved. The investment division of a large development company equips its negotiators with guidelines for explaining standard contract terms—and advice about when it's safe to deviate from them. One large insurance company has developed a strategy "playbook," a compendium of accumulated wisdom about how to negotiate with different types of clients and how to proceed in particular situations.

> Turning negotiation—often still an ad hoc process—into an organizational capability can carry a substantial ROI.

Phase V: Reviewing and Learning

The alliances group of a research and development company uses review templates to capture lessons about how it enabled or disabled effective negotiating, and also about how the other side's negotiators operated. The insights are then fed into the tools and databases the group uses to prepare for future negotiations.

Transforming negotiation from an ad hoc approach to a genuine business process can carry a substantial ROI: higher-value deals and increased chances that any given deal will stick. As one senior manager noted, "It only takes a better outcome on one multimillion dollar deal to break even on the investment—just imagine the return when we improve the results of day-to-day negotiations across the organization."

Reprint U0110E

Negotiating Under Pressure

• • •

All negotiations are challenging—but some are more difficult than others. High-pressure circumstances—for example, between stubborn or aggressive parties or during times of intense interpersonal conflict—require careful attention to relationships.

But conflict, though painful, can also lead to individual and organizational learning and growth. The selections in this part of the book offer suggestions for channeling conflict into organizationwide learning and creative resolution of problems. Guidelines for negotiating under pressure include getting to know the other party, preparing strategic moves ahead of time, and using the expression of emotion to carefully cultivate an atmosphere of cooperation.

How to Negotiate with a Hard-Nosed Adversary

• • •

Anne Field

You're about to negotiate a new contract with a major supplier, a guy with a take-no-prisoners approach who's been known to make grown men cry. But you're no wimp, so you enter the discussion ready to go *mano a mano* with your opponent, your resolve to win every bit as firm as his—and you come out with a better deal than you'd expected.

Sound like a realistic scenario? It's actually wishful thinking, according to a recent series of six studies. Researchers found that negotiators who believed they were going up against a tough opponent entered the proceedings with reduced expectations and wound up with a lower outcome than they'd predicted. In one mock 30-minute negotiation over a bonus, for example, participants who anticipated tough going wound up with $13,130, while those expecting a less competitive opponent came away with $15,540.

> When you're up against a steamroller, it's crucial to anticipate any arguments or situations that would put you in a defensive position.

"People think they will be very competitive when faced with a competitive opponent," says Kristina Diekmann, a management professor at the University of Utah's David Eccles School of Business (Salt Lake City) and a coauthor of the studies. "But when faced with the actual situation, they back down."

Why is it that a person entering a difficult negotiation doesn't rise to the occasion? Much of it has to do with motivations. People have a desire to reach agreement and avoid impasse in negotiations.

Thus, when faced with a seemingly competitive opponent, they back down to ensure agreement. Could people capitalize on this?

Yes, suggests research conducted by Diekmann and her colleagues—Ann Tenbrunsel of the University of Notre Dame's Mendoza College of Business (Notre Dame, Ind.) and Adam Galinsky of Northwestern University's Kellogg School of Management (Evanston, Ill.). Being perceived as competitive often works to your advantage. Conversely, if you assume your adversary is going to be formidable, you may respond to her in a way that encourages aggressive behavior. "It becomes a self-fulfilling prophecy," Diekmann explains.

But just being aware that your natural tendency in a tough situation may be to retreat is half the battle. Armed with that knowledge, you can take special steps to minimize the effect of your hard-nosed adversary's approach.

Get to Know Your Opponent

For starters, don't take your adversary's tough-guy reputation at face value. "The general tendency," says Diekmann, "is for people to overestimate how competitive their opponent is going to be." Try to engage your adversary in some preliminary negotiating over a relatively minor element of the process, such as where to hold the discussion. That way, you can get a feel for how flexible and friendly the individual really is.

You'd be surprised at the number of paper tigers cowering behind a scary growl. Blaine McCormick, a professor of management at Baylor University in Waco, Tex., recalls the story of a small-business owner who was trying to win parking concessions from his landlord. Not only did he want more spaces, he also wanted the landlord to stop towing unauthorized cars. When he asked other landlords in the area about their policies, he found that not only were they generally willing to make such concessions, they were also deathly afraid of legal action by business tenants. Playing a hunch, the entrepreneur started a new round of negotiations with his landlord by indicating that he was ready to go to small claims court. Lo and behold, the landlord quickly backed down.

If you've dealt with your adversary before, it's sometimes best to address his hard-nosed behavior head-on. "Usually, once you call a bully on his behavior, he stops," says Mark Gordon, a senior adviser to the Harvard Negotiation Project and director of the Boston consulting firm Vantage Partners. A misunderstanding may be the source of your opponent's aggressive style. For example, a vendor who stonewalls new contract discussions because he believes, mistakenly, that his counterpart at the manufacturing company has complained about him to his boss. Speaking directly about the perceived difficulty clears the air, in turn freeing up the negotiation process.

Reduce the One-on-One Time

If you know your opponent is a real killer, consider reducing the time you spend with her. "You want to deny them the power of in-person intimidation," says G. Richard Shell, Thomas Gerrity Professor at the Wharton School of the University of Pennsylvania (Philadelphia) and author of *Bargaining for Advantage*. Try to conduct as much business as possible through another channel—for example, e-mail or the telephone.

And don't be afraid to bring in reinforcements. "There's nothing to be gained by going in alone if you don't think you can deal with the situation," says Baylor's McCormick. Ask your boss or a colleague to join you, and suggest that the other side bring more people to the table as well. (But first do some research to determine who on the other side might best dilute your opponent's usual demeanor.)

Plan Comebacks and Strategic Moves Ahead of Time

When you're up against a steamroller, it's crucial to anticipate any arguments or situations that might put you in a defensive position. "You need comebacks that shift the opponent's perception," says Deborah M. Kolb, professor of management at the Simmons School of

Management in Boston and coauthor of *Everyday Negotiation*. She points to the background research the president of a small headhunting firm did prior to negotiating a new contract with a longtime client. During the actual negotiation, the client contended that he wasn't getting enough value for his money. But the headhunter had already researched the market to see what competitors were charging for similar services, so she confidently stood by her pricing. "Tough negotiations can take on their own momentum," Kolb says. "You need to plan ways to break it."

> Knowing your BATNA will help you avoid being browbeaten into an agreement you'll later regret.

Decide in advance how you'll buy yourself more time if things aren't going well. That means arming yourself with credible suggestions to draw on. A few examples: "I have to go back to my office for those figures," "I'll need to check with my boss first," or "I think we ought to take a break."

Another way to prevent your adversary from bullying you about time issues, especially if you're working under a tighter deadline than the other side, is to establish a longer time frame for the negotiations without revealing that you're really under the gun. (Example: "I think we'll need about a week. What do you think?") Then, if your opponent needs more time after the agreed-upon date passes, he will be at a disadvantage. After all, you both agreed to the timetable; you kept your end of the bargain. "You turn the tables on them," says Vantage Partners' Gordon.

Research the Options

It's best to avoid a situation "in which you go head-to-head on a single issue, where you dig a line in the sand and can't go any further," says Judith White, assistant professor of management at the Tuck School of Business at Dartmouth College (Hanover, N.H.).

One way to avoid such an impasse is to come prepared with various proposals—for example, a one-time agreement to supply a manufacturer with machine parts for $100,000 versus a three-year contract that grants the manufacturer a 15% discount on each shipment. By tossing out alternatives, you'll get a feel for just what your opponent's priorities are—price is rarely the only consideration. In the process of discussing alternatives, you may discover that your opponent can be more flexible than you thought.

Identify your BATNA

When you're desperate to make a deal, that weakens your bargaining position. To strengthen your hand, think through what would happen if you were unable to strike a deal. In other words, what's your BATNA? (That is, your Best Alternative to a Negotiated Agreement.) The key here is to remember that you may not be the only one who needs the deal. Do some research beforehand to see what would happen to the other side if you were to back out.

As an entertainment company executive was about to enter into negotiations with a key supplier, he learned that the vendor was going to ask for a significant increase, Gordon relates. The executive told one of his engineering teams to approach competitors about the possibility of switching the company's business. When the supplier got wind of it, they "went from feeling they had the upper hand to fearing their second-largest customer was at risk," says Gordon. In the end, the supplier asked for only a modest increase.

Knowing your BATNA makes it easy to determine the worst-case terms you'll accept, which means that you're much less likely to be browbeaten into an agreement that you'll later regret. Plus, when your opponent digs in her heels, you'll know it's time to do the same.

Bobbie Little, leader of the CEO executive coaching division of the outplacement firm DBM (New York

City), recalls a recent negotiation with a prospective client. When he refused to budge on price, says Little, "I stuck to what I knew the appropriate price should be and explained I just couldn't go below it."

When the client realized that Little was willing to end the negotiation then and there, he agreed to a higher figure. "I called his bluff," she says.

For Further Reading

Everyday Negotiation: Navigating the Hidden Agendas in Bargaining by Deborah M. Kolb and Judith Williams (2003, Jossey-Bass) *Bargaining for Advantage* by G. Richard Shell (1999, Penguin)

Reprint U0303A

Negotiating When Your Job Depends on It

You May Have to Navigate Some Tricky Interpersonal Terrain

• • •

Nick Morgan

The workplace today is a tense one. Many managers feel confronted with more conflict than ever before—and they're right. Intensified pressure to stay ahead of the competition during difficult economic times has boosted stress levels and frayed workers' nerves. But added to this source of conflict are some surprisingly potent influences that are woven into the very fabric of today's business culture.

Flatter business hierarchies and new forms of business organization are creating new opportunities for conflict in the ranks because more people throughout the company are making decisions rather than simply following orders. Meanwhile, joint ventures, partnerships, and mergers and acquisitions constantly confront employees with the need to "work out" new relationships.

Yet even as these difficulties increase, so does our dependency on one another. Few people have solitary tasks these days, and we need input and cooperation from many different people to get our jobs done. With so many diverse people and units locked in interdependency, it's inevitable that conflict will arise, conclude Sy, Barbara, and Daryl Landau, experts on negotiation and authors of *From Conflict to Creativity*.

So how can we cope with these changes in the business environment? How can we use conflict to set the stage for the kind of creative collaboration that will actually improve the status quo, not just manage a dispute? Some new work on how to negotiate under difficult conditions offers ideas for solving these modern dilemmas.

"Most of us are not comfortable with conflict, and we do not have a broad range of strategies and skills for dealing with it. We have inherited from our mammoth-hunting ancestors a fight-or-flight approach to conflict," the Landaus write. But in the work world, neither

Insights from Tough International Negotiations

Expert negotiators Michael Watkins and Susan Rosegrant, authors of *Breakthrough International Negotiation: How Great Negotiators Transformed the World's Toughest Post-Cold War Conflicts* (Jossey-Bass, 2001), look at some of the most contentious and protracted international negotiations, such as the United States–North Korea talks, to draw lessons applicable to business. "Breakthrough negotiators never view their negotiating situations as preordained or fixed. They understand that they cannot afford to get mired down in reacting to counterparts' moves," they write. "So they work to mold the basic structure of the negotiation by involving the right people, controlling the issue agenda, creating linkages that bolster their bargaining power, and channeling the flow of the process through time.

"Specifically, skilled negotiators recognize that much of what goes into shaping outcomes takes place before the parties sit down across the table from each other."

Watkins and Rosegrant offer several more principles used by what they call "breakthrough negotiators":

- **Breakthrough negotiators are organized to learn.** According to Watkins and Rosegrant, "Skilled negotiators learn by doing the necessary preparation to negotiate: they diagnose the essential features of the situation, familiarize themselves with its history and context and with the record of prior negotiations, and probe the backgrounds and reputations of their counterparts." In the case of the United States and North Korea, it was important for the U.S. team to learn about North Korea's long history of struggle not to be dominated by foreign invaders, which had given that strategically placed country a special sensitivity to matters of sovereignty. Similarly, companies with long, proud traditions of independence will face merger talks with a very different attitude than companies without such a tradition.

- **Breakthrough negotiators are masters of process design.** Given that China, Japan, South Korea, and the International Atomic Energy Association (IAEA) would all be actively involved in the negotiations, both the United States and North Korea spent a great deal of time analyzing the possible process issues. In the business world, any third parties must be considered as part of the process. For instance, when airlines and their pilots' unions talk, the negotiators must keep in mind any regulatory issues that the federal government will be monitoring.
- **Breakthrough negotiators anticipate and manage conflict.** This insight is especially important for adversaries that have a long history of conflict, such as business and labor unions. There are levels of conflict both within opposing sides and well as between them. For example, on the U.S. side in the United States–North Korea talks, the CIA and the State Department often were at odds in their opinions about how far to trust the North Koreans. Similarly, within some businesses

and unions, feeling may run high over the memories of earlier negotiations.

- **Breakthrough negotiators build momentum toward agreement.** Watkins and Rosegrant: "Negotiations do not proceed smoothly from initiation to agreement. They ebb and flow, with periods of deadlock or inaction punctuated by bursts of progress until an agreement is reached or breakdown occurs." To create pressure on the other side to close, both the United States and North Korea negotiated with the other key players in the game, including China, Japan, and the IAEA. In business, negotiating an aggressive timetable for settlement can help move the other side toward agreement.

becoming aggressive nor running away is an appropriate or effective strategy.

The Landaus say that there are basically two avenues for dealing with workplace disagreement—or any negotiation. In one, the disputed issues are addressed. For example, a manager faced with resolving a quality-control issue might ask, "Do the products need to be 100% defect-free? Or is there a certain level of error that is acceptable?"

The Landaus call this first avenue *competing*, because the two sides are competing to have their ideas put forward. One side may believe that only zero defects are tolerable, while the other may want to allow for 1% quality variance.

The second avenue for resolving work conflicts, *accommodating*, puts relationships ahead of issues, so much so that sometimes team harmony is preserved at the expense of real resolution of the problem at hand.

Most workplace negotiations favor one of these two approaches. But either approach taken alone is too limited. If you only compete, you risk damaging the relationship and thus your long-term chances for working productively with the other party. If you only accommodate, you risk compromising your own position by giving in too much for the sake of saving the relationship. You can't pursue one side to the exclusion of the other.

The experts unanimously recommend a combination approach: collaboration. As the Landaus say, "In organizations both results and relationships are important; organizations exist to produce results through the combined efforts of their members. Problems should be solved in ways that promote the competition of ideas while encouraging the cooperation of people. This is the essence of collaboration."

How can you make collaboration work for you? Marick F. Masters and Robert R. Albright, authors of *The Complete Guide to Conflict Resolution in the Workplace,* recommend following an eight-step process:

1. **Take a step back.** All too often, a lack of distance means that you are unable to grasp the entire picture. Decide on the minimum that you will accept before you walk away.

2. **Confront the situation.** Here's where you do your homework. Be brutally honest. What are the strengths of the other side's position? What are the weaknesses of yours?

3. **Sit back and listen.** Take time to listen to the other side and understand the full set of issues, wants, and wishes. Watch the body language. Don't put your position forward too early in the process.

4. **Capture the situation.** Now that you have a reasonably complete picture of the situation, it's time to make sure that everyone on your side understands it fully. Get the whole picture, not just what you want to happen.

5. **Assess and analyze.** Brainstorm possible solutions and win-win outcomes. What is the other side likely to accept? What could you stretch for?

6. **Propose possibility.** Now it's time to negotiate, using all the preparation to date. Propose an outcome that means that both sides can leave the table with success.

7. **Reach outcome.** You're probably going to have to give a little—that's just part of effective negotiation—but your work to date should make it possible for you to be happy with the end result.

8. **Build relationships.** Personal relationships should be kept separate from the negotiating points. Work to keep the connections real and positive.

Note how this process offers opportunities to compete on the ideas *and* nurture relationships.

The fight-or-flight approach to conflict may be hard-wired into our brains, but new biological research out of Emory University (Atlanta) suggests that an urge to cooperate is as well.

So when conflict arises in the workplace, as it inevitably will, give in to your best nature and take a collaborative approach to resolving it. You will avoid escalating the conflict into an all-out war. You will strengthen valuable working relationships. You will make future conflicts easier to resolve. And you could well find yourself with a solution that's more creative than what you'd initially envisioned.

For Further Reading

From Conflict to Creativity: How Resolving Workplace Disagreements Can Inspire Innovation and Productivity by Sy, Barbara, and Daryl Landau (2001, Jossey-Bass)

The Complete Guide to Conflict Resolution in the Workplace by Marick F. Masters and Robert R. Albright (2002, AMACOM)

Reprint C0209A

Transforming Negotiations

Changing Your Personal Approach to Organizational Conflict May Provide Surprising Results

• • •

Nick Morgan

It's time for another budget showdown with the marketing department. You're in charge of new product development, and for two teams answering to the same shareholders, it's amazing how many issues stand between you. They're always going on about the customer and claiming that the results of this survey or that focus group show that your new products are too far ahead of the curve. You tell them no one knew what the Walkman was before it was marketed, so how could anyone know whether they wanted one or not?

But today, the financial push has come to shove, and it's time to wrangle over next year's budget. You're thinking to yourself as you push open the glass door, "Abandon all hope ye who enter here"—the same words Dante put over the gates of hell. You know you have to negotiate, and you're afraid that Marketing is going to cite customer statistics once again as it works to take your budget away. There's no way that this is going to be a good day.

For most of us, this sort of win-lose negotiation remains our basic mental model for all kinds of conflict resolution, both personal and organizational. It's a war, or a contest, and we're the nice guy—the party of the first part who's probably going to lose. In the end, it always seems to come down to some kind of trade-off—the other guy gets more and you get less. Sure, we've all heard about win-win, but all too often the other party doesn't seem to be very interested in your half of the formula. And, in the heat of battle, it's very hard to think creatively about how it could be win-win for you to end up with a smaller budget.

But there is a better way. If, instead of thinking of conflict resolution and negotiation as an event, you begin to think of it as a journey—a transformational journey—then your perspective on this difficult, often unrewarding human activity can change. What's more, as the extensive research and writing on this topic in the last decade has shown, this way of looking at conflict resolution often works whether or not the other party is willing to play along.

Conflict is essential for both personal and organizational growth

Understood in this way, conflict and conflict resolution are the essence of organizational behavior. As experts Peter M. Kellett and Diana G. Dalton write in *Managing Conflict in a Negotiated World,* "Conflict is inherent to organizational systems. . . . Conflict is an integral part of the dynamics of how organizations manage the balances keeping them functioning effectively. First, the tensions between creativity and constraint need to be balanced. Contemporary organizations thrive and keep their employees productive when they allow them the freedom to voice experiences and the participation that stimulates creativity in employees. There is also a need for order—constraints—so creativity is directed at achieving organizational goals."

The same holds true for successful organizations as they deal with the outside world. Organizations must constantly look both toward changing their environment and being changed by it. If they can manage the former, they grow and become an established part of the marketplace. If they can manage the latter, they can change in response to the environment quickly enough to avoid the kinds of failure that more rigid organizations succumb to all too often. The truth is, as both you and Marketing know in your hearts, you're both right. Companies need both to be pulled by their customers and to push them. What you need to do is translate that fundamental truth into an ongoing budgetary "story."

At the individual level, we must all go on the same journey—balancing the need to make a mark on the world around us with the need to adjust to the reality we experience. The essence of conflict resolution involves making that collaborative journey a conscious, deliberate journey that begins with *listening*, proceeds to *learning*, then to *looking*, and finally to *leveraging* a new, creative collaboration with our partners in conflict.

Begin by rethinking your understanding of conflict and conflict resolution

Start to realize what successful conflict resolution isn't. Most of us don't like conflict, and we'd prefer that it go away from our lives. So we're tempted to pacify or placate the antagonistic ones—the squeaky wheels. What we want is adjustment of some kind to the current situation for the sake of peace. This is the kind of result you get in a budget negotiation when one party throws a tantrum. If he gets his way one time, he may well use the ploy again and again. Why not? It worked. We go along to buy peace.

When we have this attitude, we're really working toward conflict *suppression,* not resolution. But as expert negotiator and mediator Kenneth Cloke says, "Conflict suppression leads to a tolerance of evil and acceptance of injustice, which is itself repressive. The fear of change, conflict, and opposition, of standing up for what is right, of demanding what is needed, of articulating what is believed in, whether in families, organizations, or societies, leads to the overthrow of integrity and the destruction of human values."

> Creative solutions can only come from a real understanding of the common ground of both parties. That's why hard listening and learning are so important.

Neither is successful conflict resolution merely *settlement.* That's what happens when the CEO calls a halt to the shouting match between you and Marketing and says, "That's enough! I'm going to give everyone what they had last year less 3%. End of story." Cloke says, "Conflict settlement, while not actively engaged in suppressing conflict or denying its underlying causes, strives to silence outrage and enforce—through civility—a perfunctory peace. Settlement is linked with suppression through a self-replicating system.... Settlement is thus a form of suppression, and suppression a form of settlement. Those who promote suppression and settlement consider conflict an unnecessary evil."

Conflict resolution also is not *conciliation*. Conciliation is the bone that you throw to the angry parties in a dispute, by getting the other side to apologize or promise not to do the offending behavior again, or by making one side or the other take a unilateral step designed to please the opponent. Conciliation is what happens when Marketing is looking so smug, and you're so obviously unhappy, that the CEO says to the head of Marketing, "Bob, you can help this situation by agreeing to do some research on Jane's pet project. If even a few of our larger corporate customers show some interest, I'll throw some seed money at it." In other words, if suppression in conflict is a temporary cease-fire once the budget negotiation is brought to an end, then conciliation is the application of a little "hush money" to create a climate that's more appropriate to working together peacefully. Conciliation can be a useful step to take, but it is not conflict resolution and should not be mistaken as such.

Finally, conflict resolution is not *compromise*—merely splitting the difference between your budget request and Marketing's. As Cloke says, "Compromise means mutual give-and-take. There are two major problems with compromise. The first occurs when mediation becomes indistinguishable from capitulation. The second transpires when parties are asked to compromise over matters of principle, which is like advocating a happy medium between truth and lies, freedom and slavery, peace and war." If splitting the difference means that you're always forced to put off the hot new products that could potentially revolutionize the marketplace, then you understand that a series of compromises can ultimately force you to let go of a principle—or a dream.

If conflict resolution is not suppression, settlement, conciliation, or compromise, what is it? *It is collaboration to produce something new and creative—something transformational.* Cloke says, "Compromise produces results that are intermediate, lukewarm, mediocre, vague, average, and ordinary. Collaboration produces results that are unexpected, synergistic, transformational, unique, creative, and amazing. For every opposite, there are simple and complex forms of combination. Simple combination consists of adding, averaging, or blending two parts until they disappear into one. Complex combination consists of bringing opposites into creative tension and multiplying or recombining them until they become something new and different."

Steps to Conflict Resolution

How then, can you achieve collaborative conflict resolution? Here we examine the steps of the process in detail.

1: Listen carefully to both sides

Most of us seek to minimize conflict and the emotional discomfort it entails. We find it painful to listen to other points of view because we're anxious to hold on to the rightness of our own. And yet, if we're to achieve change in the situation that led to the conflict in the first place, that's precisely where we need to begin.

Cloke and Joan Goldsmith outline three important parts of good listening in their book, *Resolving Conflicts at Work: A Complete Guide for Everyone on the Job*. First, you aim to grow in understanding. "Understand the culture and the context of conflict. Discovering the meaning of the conflict, both for yourself and your adversary, leads not simply to settlement but increased awareness, acceptance, and resolution of the underlying reasons for the conflict." Next, you need to get to the heart of the matter: "Listening actively, openly, empathetically, and with your heart can take you to the center of your conflict, where all paths to resolution and transformation converge." Finally, at that heart of the conflict, you need to find the underlying emotions: "When intense emotions are brought to the surface and communicated openly and directly to the person to whom they are connected, invisible barriers are lifted to resolution and transformation."

So listen to the marketing people and ask yourself, what are the emotions underlying that apparent passion for market research? Maybe they don't have much of an understanding of what a technical breakthrough your latest ideas represent.

Listening during conflict involves listening to both sides—to your own as well as to the other side. It's only through this kind of intense, honest involvement that you can begin to understand not only the ground that you stand on, and that your opponent stands on, but the ground that underlies you both. That's where the beginnings of collaboration can be found. Aren't you both, at base, seeking to delight your customers? Why does that basic desire play out in such different ways in practice?

Understanding the language of the conflict—both yours and your opponent's—is crucial to the transformational process. Do you use the language of war—"They shot down every idea as fast as we put them up"? Do you use the language of competition—"Their team isn't playing by the rules"? Or the language of the journey—"Can we take this one step together"? The kind of language you and the other side use can both signal and even control behavior during negotiation. If your language signals deep, unspoken doubts about the other side's willingness to truly engage in a solution, then those assumptions need to be fully aired, or they will get in the way of any possible collaboration. The same, of course, goes for the other side.

2: Learn about the underlying causes of the conflict

Once you've begun to understand what makes both sides tick by listening carefully to the stated positions and the language with which those positions are stated, it's time to figure out what you can do about the situation. You need to get beneath the emotions to learn what makes those emotions strong and enduring. What are the underlying fears that give rise to all the impediments to a solution? What underlies those surveys and focus groups you're always teasing Marketing about? Could it be you're both baffled by the whims of an increasingly finicky consumer?

When these feelings are clear, you can begin to separate the positional wheat from the chaff. As Cloke and Goldsmith say, "Separate what matters from what's in the way. The road to resolution and transformation lies not in debate over who is right but in dialogue, not in competition over positions but collaboration to satisfy mutual needs." Key to this growing comprehension, say Cloke and Goldsmith, is learning from difficult behaviors. "In every conflict we confront difficult behaviors that provide us with opportunities to improve our skills and develop our capacity for empathy, patience, and perseverance."

Cloke and Goldsmith identify six layers beneath the apparent issues of any conflict: personalities; emotions; interests, needs, and desires; self-perceptions and self-esteem; hidden expectations; and unresolved issues from the past. Others might be found, but in learning about this "iceberg" of hidden levers in conflict resolution, you will find the beginnings of a transformational way out of the dilemma. Each of these layers, if poorly understood or ignored, can block any hope of resolution. Are the personalities of the participants fundamentally different? Does one party harbor deep unacknowledged anger toward the other party? What does each party really want out of the conflict? What do you understand your own strengths and weaknesses to be? What false expectations do you or your opponents have for the outcome of this conflict? And finally, are you (or your opponents) really fighting another battle all over again, one from the past, where things didn't turn out as you had hoped? Is this really all about that product failure from a few years back that you still don't like to talk about? The one that Marketing bet heavily on and then had to abandon halfway through the biggest campaign it had ever launched?

Answering these questions honestly and deeply about both you and your opponents is extraordinarily difficult, yet essential if your conflict resolution is to be transformational.

3: Look for creative ways to move along your path to resolution

When we look deeply enough into our own motivations and desires, we will almost always find ambiguity and paradox. Confronting those paradoxes can be painful, but it is part of developing solutions for the most difficult issues in conflict resolution. This is essentially a problem-solving process: ultimately you know you have to become more customer-focused, but you don't want to let go of your passion for top-quality product engineering. How will you resolve this paradox?

First, you must accept the paradoxes you find and create positive energy around creative responses to them. Next, you need to figure out how to solve the problems you've discovered. As Cloke and Goldsmith say, "There are many approaches we can take to solving our problems, but most of us approach them with the attitude that they are adversaries or enemies that need to be defeated or controlled, rather than seeing them as opportunities for learning and improvement. We face problems all our lives, but only rarely do we stop to consider how we can improve the way we go about trying to solve them."

> Understanding the language of the conflict—both yours and your opponent's— is crucial to the transformational process.

Are there some other, less confrontational ways to approach the problem together with Marketing? Could you bring some major customers into your R & D process?

This step is the heart of the transformational journey of successful conflict resolution. If you can find creative solutions to the core problems you've uncovered through deeply attentive listening and learning, you will have mastered the most difficult part of getting to resolution. Here is where your command of the collaboration is truly tested. Creative solutions can only come from a real understanding of the common ground of both parties. That's why hard listening and learning are so important.

4: Leverage the understanding you've gained to develop action

Once you've designed your brilliant solutions to the hitherto intractable problems you've newly understood, you still have to persuade both parties to act on your solutions. Here, you need to leverage the understanding and trust you've established to persuade the participants to let go of the status quo and move on.

Conflicts are opportunities for personal and organizational growth. They are not often simple, and rarely tension-free, but they hold within them the possibilities of enormous creativity and progress. The alternative is stagnation—and a nagging feeling that you and the marketing department are leaving a lot of good ideas on the table—for your competitors to pick up and act on.

For Further Reading

Managing Conflict in a Negotiated World by Peter M. Kellett and Diana G. Dalton (2001, Sage Publications)

Resolving Conflicts at Work: A Complete Guide for Everyone on the Job by Kenneth Cloke and Joan Goldsmith (2000, Jossey-Bass)

Reprint C0112A

Expert Negotiating

G. Richard Shell Tells How to Win the Game Every Time

* * *

Most businesspeople can become better negotiators by learning a few basic skills, says G. Richard Shell, author of *Bargaining for Advantage: Negotiation Strategies for Reasonable People*. Shell is founder and academic director of the Wharton Executive Negotiation Workshop at the Wharton School of the University of Pennsylvania in Philadelphia. He has coached executives in a wide variety of professions and is chair of the legal studies department at Wharton, where *HMCL* contributing writer Jeffrey Marshall recently interviewed him.

If you're a type A personality, why shouldn't you try to suddenly be a pussycat?

Shell: We've found that training people without respecting their different personality types is very unsuccessful. We start by assessing people's attitudes toward interpersonal conflict, and their attitudes about negotiation. We want to expand the set of communication skills that are authentically their own. If you're a very cooperative person, and you find yourself in a nail-biting, hard negotiation situation, the chances are that you won't be very successful.

There may be situations where you'd want to bring in additional resources, or actually turn the negotiation over to someone else who is more competitive. Very often a competitive person will understand what's going on in the mind of another competitive person, while for a cooperative person, it's all very mysterious, and very upsetting.

Are there personality traits and communication skills that prove especially helpful for the novice negotiator?

Shell: Willingness to listen, whether in competitive or cooperative people—and both types can be good listeners, depending on the situation—is a key skill. That technique is relatively easy to teach. Still, competitive people tend to listen just long enough to get their next angle, and then they're off to the races.

The key to understanding whether or not you're up against a competitive person is whether they reciprocate. If you hit the ball over the net and it doesn't come back, then you're up against a competitive negotiator, and you need to make an adjustment.

How important are nonverbal manifestations like body language and eye contact in a negotiation?

Shell: I think they're very important, but we've found that focusing on those aspects of negotiation as a teaching method is counterproductive. You're paying more attention to the box than what's in the box.

Should we all be actors, and conceal our emotions when someone throws us a curve?

Shell: It always helps to be in control of your emotions, but it can also be effective to express them. We like to say: Use your temper, don't lose it. As far as acting is concerned, we try to teach people to be themselves as negotiators.

Should you ever threaten your opponent?

Shell: Threats are very interesting negotiation options. The implicit notion that you have something to take away from the other person is a vital aspect of negotiations, and you have to be comfortable with that power on your side of the table, or you're not going to be very successful.

To actually make a threat explicit is a very strong bargaining move, and we recommend reserving it for one of two situations. First, if you're up against a competitive negotiator, and he's threatening you early in the process, you have to show that you can threaten him, too. Then there's been reciprocity on that issue, and everyone knows they can hurt each other. We call it "matching" your counterpart's style if they show a needlessly aggressive opening.

The other time when threats are required is at the end of the process, when you've exhausted all of the positive leverage you may have, and the other party is not acting in what you think are really their own best interests. You need to show them that the world without this opportunity really looks grim. Then they often will come around.

For example, litigation can be used as a threat. In Japan, this would be explosive. But in American business, litigation is as normal as driving. When you say, "If you do this, we'll have to sue you," that's a threat, but it's not the end of the world to a business relationship in the U.S.

Why are great negotiators good listeners and why do they ask a lot of questions?

Shell: The average negotiators focus on themselves—their problems, their goals, their perceptions of the world. Highly skilled negotiators focus on the other party. They've done all the homework on their own piece, and they've got a boatload of questions in mind. All the assumptions we make about how the world looks to the other side, in a skilled negotiator's hands, are subjects of inquiry. I think the single most important attribute of a great negotiator is the willingness to be ignorant, or assume a role of ignorance.

> "Ask yourself, 'Who am I, who are they, and what will it take to persuade them?' Whatever it takes, that's what you do."

You say, "Don't haggle when you should negotiate." What do you mean by that?

Shell: Sometimes people say, "Okay, you start at 10, and I start at five, and we end up at seven and a half." People will import that model into situations that are much more complicated. There may be five issues, not just one. There may be relationship matters at stake as well. Negotiation involves the exploration of all the alternative solutions that might exist, including the mid-point. But if you have five issues and you simply go through them one at a time, and say, "What's your position on this issue? Well, here's my position, and let's split the difference," that's haggling. You're going to find you leave a lot of money on the table, because it's very likely that of those issues, one or two are vitally important to you, and the others are not. You'd be much better off giving them everything on one of your less important issues, and getting everything on another issue that you want, and then splitting the difference on one or two others.

If you're on a team of negotiators, how important is it to have consistent communication?

Shell: It's absolutely vital, and it's something that many firms don't train their people to do. Firms will spend hundreds of thousands of dollars training people on sales or even on negotiations, then put them on teams and send them out to negotiate together, and give them no training at all in terms of team dynamics. And it's usually the highest-stakes deal that calls for a team.

Isn't it fairly uncommon to have a written goal, and communicate it with someone else so you're not flying solo?

Shell: Yes. Basically, people wing it. Research on negotiation shows that you can get by with that, but you're leaving enormous amounts of potential advantage on the table by not spending time thinking more carefully about a specific aspiration and justifying it in your mind. This is particularly true for cooperative types, who make a lot of concessions to the other party before they actually start negotiating.

Commitment to your own goals is very important. Research has shown that if you write things down, you become slightly more committed to them because they've become objectified. One further step is to express the goal to someone else, even if it's your spouse or your teammate, because then you have an audience you're accountable to.

Does the skillful negotiator figure out which lever is stronger for him?

Shell: I think so. If you keep your goals firmly in mind, then as you go through the negotiation, the best way to persuade the other party that your goals are justified, and are within their interests, will occur to you. At the workshop, we often say that the shortest form of negotiation preparation you can engage in is to ask yourself, "Who am I, who are they, and what will it take to persuade them?" Whatever it takes, that's what you do.

Most professional people are not natural negotiators, especially in America, where we're not a haggling culture. Getting information and knowledge about the process, so that you gain confidence and become intellectually comfortable with it, is an incredibly important tool to add to your professional toolbox. Even getting a little better at negotiation can yield enormous benefits to the bottom line and to your own rewards.

For Further Reading

Bargaining for Advantage: Negotiation Strategies for Reasonable People by G. Richard Shell (1999, Viking)

Reprint C9912B

Negotiating Across Cultures

• • •

Perhaps the biggest threat to the positive relationships required for any successful negotiation comes with cross-cultural bargaining—when the potential for misunderstanding and confusion rises sharply. As businesses from around the world increasingly interact with one another, the ability to engage in skillful collaborative negotiation is more important than ever.

The articles in this section explain some of the common pitfalls in cross-cultural negotiation and offer suggestions for avoiding them. The best bargainers understand that people from different cultures can have very different ideas about how long a negotiation should take, how important the relationship is compared to the details of the deal, and what constitutes proper preparation for a bargaining session. Skilled negotiators also understand different decision-making styles, look for common ground, and adroitly prevent themselves from being manipulated by their counterparts' tactics.

How to Avoid Being the "Ugly American" When Doing Business Abroad

* * *

Andrew Rosenbaum

You know the stereotype: They're bold, brash, and all business. They've got lots of money but little culture. They're immune to self-doubt and oblivious to cultural nuance.

They're the Ugly Americans.

The 1958 book and 1963 film adaptation gave the stereotype its name. How closely does the stereotype fit the reality of Americans doing business abroad today? How "ugly" are American businesspeople as they work with foreign partners in this our globalized world?

"Americans have a much greater willingness to adapt to other cultures than they did when that book was written," says Prabhu Guptara, director of the Executive Development Centre for UBS bank in Wolfsberg, Switzerland. "But Americans often still need to improve self-consciousness to understand that the qualities that make you win in the U.S. could as easily make you fail in Europe or Asia."

American execs need to be especially sensitive about three aspects of communications when they go abroad:

1. **The rhythm of negotiations.** Speed and directness are not necessarily qualities that foreigners appreciate, even though Americans like them.

2. **The dynamics of personal relationships.** Business in most of the developed world is people-based, not deal-based, so don't parachute in with the "lawyers and the dollars."

3. **The depth of presentation.** Slick speeches and PowerPoint slide shows may not get you far in cultures that value depth. You'd better have all the numbers and know what they mean.

Why these areas in particular? "Because Americans tend to value fast and agile dealmaking, and intense and skilled marketing, while not putting much value on personal relationships in business," explains Ann McDonagh Bengtsson, a France-based international consultant specializing in change management, especially where a number of different cultures are involved. "Whereas, most Europeans and many Asians want to develop a solid personal relationship before even considering a deal, and then expect very detailed and painstaking research to have gone into the preparation of any accord," Bengtsson says.

Says Japanese intercultural expert Shinobu Kitayama: "American culture emphasizes the core cultural idea of independence by valuing attending to oneself and discovering and expressing individual qualities while neither assuming nor valuing overt connectedness. These values are reflected in educational and legal systems, employment and caretaking practices, and individual cognition, emotion, and motivation."

In contrast, Bengtsson and Kitayama argue that Asian and European cultures tend to emphasize interdependence by valuing the self and individuality within a social context, connections among persons, and attending to and harmoniously coordinating with others. When Kitayama asked 65 middle-class American and 90 Japanese students attending the same Oregon university to list situations in which they felt that they were winning or losing, the American students focused more on ways in which they won individually, while the Japanese students won when the group with which they were associated enjoyed a success.

American execs abroad have to take these differences into account. So, when abroad

Slow Down

The rhythm of negotiations and all business discussion is much slower outside the United States, as executives from the New York–based Bankers Trust had to learn when it merged with the Frankfurt-based Deutsche Bank two years ago.

Deutsche Bank was a very large, "universal" bank, as the Germans call such an entity. The bank was active in all sectors of banking, but the area where it needed the most reinforcement was investment banking. Hence the plan to merge with investment house Bankers Trust, a dedicated merchant bank with an American, "deals-based" culture.

The American executives quickly found that they could not fathom their German partners, reports international management professor Terry Garrison of the Henley Management College (Henley-on-Thames, England). "Accustomed to making split-second decisions, and managing on a project basis in which planning rarely extended beyond a given deal, the Bankers Trust 'hot-shots' found themselves working with 'universal' bankers who planned several years at a time, for whom a given 'deal' was something they felt they could take or leave, and who operated within a corporate governance framework that looked and felt completely alien to the Americans."

> Forcing a conclusion with a foreign partner can only cause problems.

Garrison ran a seminar in which he helped the American execs get in tune with Continental banking culture. "It was a matter of teaching the Americans to slow down and think in different terms," Garrison says. "Those Germans who had spent a lifetime in a credit-management culture saw themselves as needing not just a crash course in merchant banking but a whole new vocabulary rooted in American capitalism."

Deutsche Bank executive Siegfried Guterman admits that "there were a lot of unmeasurable factors that were difficult to take into account before we accomplished the merger."

It is not that Asians and European cultures do not value efficiency. Rather, business for them is more conceptual and long-term. A given transaction is only interesting if it is part of the accomplishment of a much more stable, greater objective. "Attempts to hurry your foreign interlocutors along may just make them withdraw from the discussions altogether," Bengtsson points out.

Don't Arrive with "the Lawyers and the Dollars"

Personal and business relationships are more intertwined in Europe and in Asia that they are in the United States.

"Achieving trust with European and Asian partners is a key factor in success outside the U.S.," Guptara says. "Americans may not like each other, but if there is a 'deal' on the table, they do business. Most Asians and Europeans—even the British—want to get to know you first. They want to assure themselves that you are reliable, that you will not only go the distance for them this time, but that you will be there to do it again when they call upon you."

So, take the time to go for lunch with your prospective business partners abroad. Don't talk business right away—ask them about what things are like in their country. Find something that you have in common with them. Maybe you both like a certain sport? Perhaps you share an interest in Italian wine?

During this time, you can observe your interlocutor's reactions. What makes him laugh? Does he react with hostility to certain kinds of expressions? "When you get around to dessert, bring up the subject of the business at hand in a very casual way. Get some indications from his reaction about how to proceed. But let your interlocutor lead you through it all," says Guptara.

Negotiating experts agree that forcing a conclusion with a foreign partner can only cause problems. "Don't be afraid to drop the matter and to talk about the weather," says Garrison. "Don't be too serious, especially at the outset. Show your interlocutor that you are in no hurry to conclude, and he will assume that you are serious. Insist on a conclusion, and he will assume that you are desperate."

Establishing trust is a factor that an American businessperson abroad must take into account not only in negotiations, but also in working with Europeans or Asians on a day-to-day basis.

Disney had to endure an expensive lesson of this type when it opened EuroDisney outside Paris. The management expected the French employees to conform to American expectations in their work, and did little to build up trust. A long and agonizing conflict with French labor unions was the only result of this policy. Finally, Disney gave up and hired French managers. Labor difficulties were smoothed out when managers and workers began to trust each other.

Get the Details Right

Although the British may accept a slick PR demo while negotiating, most of the cultures on the Continent and many in Asia do not.

"There is a real academic side to business in Europe and in parts of Asia," Guptara says. "A business presentation to such interlocutors is like defending a Ph.D. thesis. They expect you to have real depth, all the numbers, and to be able to answer every question. Fail at this and they will never trust you. The word that Europeans apply to a businessman who can't answer key questions is *liar*."

It may seem useless pedantry on the part of your prospective business partners to insist on great detail, "but their view is that the details are the easy part," says Bengtsson. "And a thoroughness in knowledge of your subject means—especially to Europeans, rightly or wrongly—that the risks are being adequately managed."

One American manufacturer recently hit all the wrong buttons in discussions with a French acquisition. Arriving in Paris, the American company promptly invited the board of the French company to lunch. The French board was of the most traditional sort—all graduates of the *grandes écoles*, they perceived themselves to be fashionable, witty, and cultivated.

When the French businessmen arrived at the lunch, they were astonished to find their American colleagues wearing baseball hats and T-shirts with the name of the acquiring company on them. There was also a pile of such hats and shirts on the table, and they were bidden to put them on.

This suggestion did not go over well. But even worse was the period at lunch when the French—after what they thought was a decent delay—began asking strategic questions. It became obvious that the American executives knew little or nothing about the company they were acquiring apart from its balance sheet.

After that, the massive departure of the French businessmen from the company should not have taken the Americans by surprise.

Play by the Rules — Their Rules

When an American executive goes abroad, it's very easy for cultural assumptions to slip into her suitcase. "When negotiations are prolonged, or frustrating, these cultural assumptions tend to jump out of the suitcase, onto the negotiating table," Bengtsson points out. The point to remember at times like this is that you are in someone else's culture and, for the time being, you need to play by their rules.

Because of tighter budgets, companies are sending fewer executives abroad these days, so the executive who is sent to a foreign country has mission-critical work to do. Thus it's essential that the executive adapt to a different culture's rules: for communication, interaction, and negotiation. If he doesn't, if he acts the proverbial "Ugly American," his chances for success are small.

Reprint C0212C

How to Steer Clear of Pitfalls in Cross-Cultural Negotiation

• • •

Andrew Rosenbaum

Henry in Los Angeles and Hiroshi in Tokyo both like Armani suits, baseball, Mozart, and good Bordeaux. But Henry recently spoke for days with Hiroshi, his potential business partner, and yet the barriers between them were never broached—and the deal didn't get inked.

The problem had to do with different conceptions of the negotiation process itself and misinterpretations of the other's behavior. For Henry, negotiation is about pushing through a deal, period. When Henry didn't think their discussion was moving forward as quickly as he thought it should, his arguments became increasingly forceful. Because Hiroshi read this as disrespect, the negotiation essentially ended days before their talks did.

Although globalized communications and marketing have made the world smaller in many ways, deep differences between cultures remain. Despite similar tastes, Henry and Hiroshi each approach negotiation in a way heavily conditioned by his national culture. Because they sat down at the table without understanding the other's assumptions about the negotiation process, all they ended up with was an impasse.

Negotiation is always a delicate business, requiring determination and diplomacy in equal measure. But finessing a cross-cultural negotiation is a particular challenge. Here are some tips that can help you put together a deal with a foreign partner.

Understand Expectations

Your negotiating partner's expectations of the negotiation may well be very different from yours. Like you, he will want to succeed, but success may not mean the same thing to him and his conationals as it does to you.

Decision-making styles may be different, too. American managers usually make decisions by themselves,

Is Intercultural Negotiation Different on the Net?

Only in part, say Gregory E. Kersten of the J. Molson School of Business in Concordia, Canada, and Sabine T. Köszegi and Rudolf Vetschera of the University of Vienna, who together conducted an e-negotiation study. Odd as it may seem, given that Net correspondents usually cannot see their interlocutors, cultural factors affect e-negotiations almost as much as they do traditional ones, the study shows.

"In face-to-face negotiations subjects may modify their behavior and attitudes according to their perceptions of the counterparts' culture. In anonymous negotiations, participants cannot rely on these clues and thus are more likely to base their behavior on scripts inherent to their own culture," write the authors.

while Japanese managers tend to make decisions by consensus, a practice that can add time to the negotiation process. Americans place a high value on flexibility, whereas once a Japanese manager has reached a decision, he believes it is shameful to change it, says Tokyo-based management consultant Mitsugu Iwashita, director of the Intercultural and Business Communication Center. Understanding these underlying attitudes helps you see what your potential partner's priorities are, and you can then adapt your strategy accordingly.

Establish Common Ground
and Choose Your Style

Find anything that will allow your foreign colleague to share something with you. This can help you get past "people" problems—ego wars, saving face, and so on—which is a good tactic because these problems can crop up where you may least expect them.

Now the real work can begin. You'll need to choose which of two classic negotiating styles you'll adopt: Contentious or problem-solving. The contentious negotiator, a tough, demanding guy who makes few compromises, can be a great success given the right conditions. He either wins or loses, but never comes to a conditional agreement. The problem-solving negotiator takes a broader view, attempting to get as much as she can without handing out a dealbreaker. She establishes common ground wherever she can find it and approaches negotiations on a step-by-step basis.

While one has to be careful about generalizing across cultures, experts agree that a problem-solving approach to cross-cultural negotiations is prudent. (Indeed, many would say it's the right choice for almost any negotiation.) The problem-solving approach helps to avoid blunders, says Elaine Winters, coauthor of *Cultural Issues in Business Communication* (Program Facilitating and Consulting, 2000).

But there are limits to this approach. In many cultures, negotiation is ritualized, especially in its early stages. It is obviously important to learn these negotiating rituals for a given culture, even if your foreign partner turns out not to require them. Germans, for example, often need to spend a large part of the initial negotiations in number crunching. All the facts and figures must be agreed upon, and woe betide the negotiator who makes a mistake! This German trait is not really about number-crunching, however; it is a confidence-building ritual in which two potential partners run through a series of routine checks just to display trustworthiness. So the problem-solving approach, which would try to find common ground quickly, could prove threatening for the ritual negotiators.

"When confronted with cultural differences in negotiating styles, we need to be aware of the potentially adverse effects of a flexible, mixed style," says Willem Mastenbroek, director of the Holland Consulting Group (Amsterdam) and professor of organizational culture and communication at the Free University of Amsterdam. "If it is not understood, people may perceive it as smooth and suave behavior and resent it. Because they are not able to counter it with equal flexibility, they may feel clumsy and awkward, in some way even inferior. It may also become difficult for them to believe in the sincerity of the other side. They may see it as an effort to lure them into a game defined by established groups which will put them at a disadvantage."

Manage the Negotiation

Let's assume that you have passed successfully through the initial stages of the negotiation and that you have agreed upon common ground with your prospective partner. The game of tactics now broadens. It is at this stage, in which the actual issues go back and forth between participants, that your awareness of negotiating behavior typical to your potential partner's culture can be put to use.

Italian negotiators, for example, will often try to push through this stage quite quickly, repeatedly insisting on their terms to tire out their opponents. Knowing this, a foreign negotiator may find a good tactic is to display no great hurry to deal—change the subject, digress, etc.

On the other hand, Chinese negotiators usually make one offer after another at this point to test the limits of a possible deal. According to Winters, nonverbal communication in negotiations with a Chinese businessman can be quite important. He may say little in response to your questions, and expect you to garner what you need to know from his gestures and from the context of whatever he does say. More demonstrative Western cultures can find this conduct very difficult to work with, but the application here of patience and deductive reasoning can take you a long way.

Most Europeans won't break off discussions unless they are deeply offended, but Asian negotiators are often happy to drop the project if they are uncomfortable with some aspect of the negotiations. If this happens, try to backtrack and fix the problem.

But in focusing on your potential partner's culture, don't lose sight of him as an individual. It's always best to learn as much as you can about his personality and communication style. "Personalize negotiation methods and approaches," Winters says. "Don't ignore culture (impossible anyway!), try to treat it as background; focus on the capabilities of the specific individuals at the table. This is frequently successful because a new, mutually agreed-upon culture is being created just for this effort."

Reprint C0303B

About the Contributors

Tom Krattenmaker is a Philadelphia-area author and the director of news and information at Swarthmore College.

Rebecca M. Saunders is a freelance writer based in New York City.

Nick Wreden is the author of *Fusion Branding: Strategic Branding for the Customer Economy*. He is also a consultant based in Atlanta.

Marjorie Corman Aaron is a freelance writer.

Stephen Bernhut is a Toronto-based editor who writes about business and management.

Jeff Weiss is founder and director of Vantage Partners, a consulting firm based in Boston.

Anne Field is a Pelham, N.Y.–based business writer.

Nick Morgan is a former editor at *Harvard Management Update*.

Andrew Rosenbaum is a *Time* magazine correspondent in Amsterdam. He also writes regularly on European financial and management issues for specialized publications.

Harvard Business Review Paperback Series

The Harvard Business Review Paperback Series offers the best thinking on cutting-edge management ideas from the world's leading thinkers, researchers, and managers. Designed for leaders who believe in the power of ideas to change business, these books will be useful to managers at all levels of experience, but especially senior executives and general managers. In addition, this series is widely used in training and executive development programs.

Books are priced at $19.95 U.S.
Price subject to change.

Title	Product #
Harvard Business Review **Interviews with CEOs**	3294
Harvard Business Review on **Advances in Strategy**	8032
Harvard Business Review on **Becoming a High Performance Manager**	1296
Harvard Business Review on **Brand Management**	1445
Harvard Business Review on **Breakthrough Leadership**	8059
Harvard Business Review on **Breakthrough Thinking**	181X
Harvard Business Review on **Building Personal and Organizational Resilience**	2721
Harvard Business Review on **Business and the Environment**	2336
Harvard Business Review on **Change**	8842
Harvard Business Review on **Compensation**	701X
Harvard Business Review on **Corporate Ethics**	273X
Harvard Business Review on **Corporate Governance**	2379
Harvard Business Review on **Corporate Responsibility**	2748
Harvard Business Review on **Corporate Strategy**	1429
Harvard Business Review on **Crisis Management**	2352
Harvard Business Review on **Culture and Change**	8369
Harvard Business Review on **Customer Relationship Management**	6994
Harvard Business Review on **Decision Making**	5572
Harvard Business Review on **Effective Communication**	1437

To order, call 1-800-668-6780, or go online at www.HBSPress.org

Title	Product #
Harvard Business Review on **Entrepreneurship**	9105
Harvard Business Review on **Finding and Keeping the Best People**	5564
Harvard Business Review on **Innovation**	6145
Harvard Business Review on **Knowledge Management**	8818
Harvard Business Review on **Leadership**	8834
Harvard Business Review on **Leadership at the Top**	2756
Harvard Business Review on **Leading in Turbulent Times**	1806
Harvard Business Review on **Managing Diversity**	7001
Harvard Business Review on **Managing High-Tech Industries**	1828
Harvard Business Review on **Managing People**	9075
Harvard Business Review on **Managing the Value Chain**	2344
Harvard Business Review on **Managing Uncertainty**	9083
Harvard Business Review on **Managing Your Career**	1318
Harvard Business Review on **Marketing**	8040
Harvard Business Review on **Measuring Corporate Performance**	8826
Harvard Business Review on **Mergers and Acquisitions**	5556
Harvard Business Review on **Motivating People**	1326
Harvard Business Review on **Negotiation**	2360
Harvard Business Review on **Nonprofits**	9091
Harvard Business Review on **Organizational Learning**	6153
Harvard Business Review on **Strategic Alliances**	1334
Harvard Business Review on **Strategies for Growth**	8850
Harvard Business Review on **The Business Value of IT**	9121
Harvard Business Review on **The Innovative Enterprise**	130X
Harvard Business Review on **Turnarounds**	6366
Harvard Business Review on **What Makes a Leader**	6374
Harvard Business Review on **Work and Life Balance**	3286

Management Dilemmas: Case Studies from the Pages of Harvard Business Review

How often do you wish you could turn to a panel of experts to guide you through tough management situations? The Management Dilemmas series provides just that. Drawn from the pages of *Harvard Business Review,* each insightful volume poses several perplexing predicaments and shares the problem-solving wisdom of leading experts. Engagingly written, these solutions-oriented collections help managers make sound judgment calls when addressing every-day management dilemmas.

These books are priced at $19.95 U.S.
Price subject to change.

Title	Product #
Management Dilemmas: **When Change Comes Undone**	5038
Management Dilemmas: **When Good People Behave Badly**	5046
Management Dilemmas: **When Marketing Becomes a Minefield**	290X

To order, call 1-800-668-6780, or go online at www.HBSPress.org

Harvard Business Essentials

In the fast-paced world of business today, everyone needs a personal resource—a place to go for advice, coaching, background information, or answers. The Harvard Business Essentials series fits the bill. Concise and straightforward, these books provide highly practical advice for readers at all levels of experience. Whether you are a new manager interested in expanding your skills or an experienced executive looking to stay on top, these solution-oriented books give you the reliable tips and tools you need to improve your performance and get the job done. Harvard Business Essentials titles will quickly become your constant companions and trusted guides.

These books are priced at $19.95 U.S., except as noted.
Price subject to change.

Title	Product #
Harvard Business Essentials: **Negotiation**	1113
Harvard Business Essentials: **Managing Creativity and Innovation**	1121
Harvard Business Essentials: **Managing Change and Transition**	8741
Harvard Business Essentials: **Hiring and Keeping the Best People**	875X
Harvard Business Essentials: **Finance**	8768
Harvard Business Essentials: **Business Communication**	113X
Harvard Business Essentials: **Manager's Toolkit ($24.95)**	2896
Harvard Business Essentials: **Managing Projects Large and Small**	3213
Harvard Business Essentials: **Creating Teams with an Edge**	290X

The Results-Driven Manager

The Results-Driven Manager series collects timely articles from *Harvard Management Update* and *Harvard Management Communication Letter* to help senior to middle managers sharpen their skills, increase their effectiveness, and gain a competitive edge. Presented in a concise, accessible format to save managers valuable time, these books offer authoritative insights and techniques for improving job performance and achieving immediate results.

These books are priced at $14.95 U.S.
Price subject to change.

Title	Product #
The Results-Driven Manager:	
Face-to-Face Communications for Clarity and Impact	3477
The Results-Driven Manager:	
Managing Yourself for the Career You Want	3469
The Results-Driven Manager:	
Presentations That Persuade and Motivate	3493
The Results-Driven Manager: **Teams That Click**	3507
The Results-Driven Manager:	
Winning Negotiations That Preserve Relationships	3485

To order, call 1-800-668-6780, or go online at www.HBSPress.org

Readers of the Results-Driven Manager series find the following Harvard Business School Press books of interest.

If you find these books useful:	You may also like these:
Presentations That Persuade and Motivate	Working the Room (8199)
Face-to-Face Communications for Clarity and Impact	HBR on Effective Communication (1437) HBR on Managing People (9075)
Winning Negotiations That Preserve Relationships	HBR on Negotiation (2360) HBE Guide to Negotiation (1113)
Teams That Click	The Wisdom of Teams (3670) Leading Teams (3332)
Managing Yourself for the Career You Want	Primal Leadership (486X) Leading Quietly (4878) Leadership on the Line (4371)